University of
California Press
Berkeley
and Los Angeles
1951

MANUAL OF AMERICAN ENGLISH PRONUNCIATION

for adult foreign students

by

Clifford H. Prator, Jr.

University of California Press
Berkeley and Los Angeles California

Cambridge University Press
London, England

Copyright, 1951, by
The Regents of the University of California

Second Printing, 1953

ACKNOWLEDGMENTS

The author is glad to express his deep gratitude to the following persons and organizations:

Professor Franklin P. Rolfe, Divisional Dean of Humanities and former Chairman of the Department of English at the University of California, Los Angeles, who gave every facility and encouragement for the development of this textbook project.

Miss Margaret L. Wotton, Principal Extension Representative, who first suggested that classes taught in University Extension might be used as a testing ground for the *Manual*, and offered help in financing preliminary printings.

Mr. Bernard M. Goldman, Mr. Reed Lawton, Mr. Morris V. Jones, and Mrs. Merle McCrae, the teachers who tried out the materials in their classes and carefully reported the results.

Professor Albert H. Marckwardt of the University of Michigan, who was willing to help think through many of the problems of the text.

The U. S. Educational Foundation in the Philippines, which administered a Fulbright Grant because of which the work was finished much earlier than would otherwise have been possible.

> C. H. P. Jr.
> Manila, Republic of the Philippines
> February, 1950

CONTENTS

Introduction: To the Teacher

Lesson

I.	The Phonetic Alphabet	1
II.	Classification of Vowels	10
III.	Unstressed Vowels	16
IV.	Sentence-Stress and Rhythm	23
V.	Rising-Falling Intonation	38
VI.	Rising Intonation	51
VII.	Classification of Consonants; the Endings -s and -ed	69
VIII.	Initial and Final Consonants	78
IX.	L, R, and Syllabic Consonants	89
X.	Front Vowels	99
XI.	Back Vowels	109
XII.	"Long" and "Short" Vowels	119
XIII.	Spelling and Vowel Sounds	129
XIV.	Consonant Substitutions: I ([t], [θ], [d], [ð]; [dʒ], [y]; and [ʃ], [tʃ])	143
XV.	Consonant Substitutions: II ([b], [v], [w], [hw]; [n], [ŋ], [ŋk]; and [h])	152

Accent Inventory (separate pamphlet)

INTRODUCTION TO THE TEACHER

I. **What the Manual Is.**

As the international activities and responsibilities of the United States increase, so does the concern of our government and our educators for the teaching of English as a second language. Since World War II the number of students from abroad in American institutions of higher learning has risen from some 6,000 to nearly 25,000, enough to make up one of the world's largest universities. Each year more institutions, even the smaller ones, find it advisable to set up special courses in English as a foreign language. The current influx of new citizens under the Displaced Persons Act is making it necessary for our city school systems to create new Americanization and language classes. In many countries the U. S. Department of State has opened cultural institutes and libraries to which students flock in great numbers to learn English; and more such centers are contemplated. Each effort of our government to give technological aid to backward regions means that a new group of foreign technicians must be trained, either in this country or abroad, in the language that will make the exchange of information possible. Owing to the increased prestige of the United States as a center of scientific, industrial, and even cultural progress, educational institutions throughout much of the world are showing an unaccustomed interest in American English.

Unfortunately, the production of adequate teaching materials for use in this type of instruction has fallen far behind the demand. Anyone who has talked to teachers of English as a second language in recent years knows how continuous and generally unsuccessful has been their search for textbooks prepared to meet their special needs. All sorts of make-shifts are being used: improvised lesson sheets, Americanization texts from the days when there were no immigration quotas, books intended for native-born speakers of English.

Materials for teaching pronunciation are no exception to the general rule. Some instructors have been forced to adopt the very fine British texts which were a by-product of the Empire's long career as the world's leading international power, though in no respect do American and British vary so widely as in pronunciation. Others are attempting to use speech correction manuals prepared for the typical American undergraduate. These, with their literary readings, their emphasis on isolated sounds, their treatment of all sounds and combinations as of equal importance, their preoccupation with clarity of articulation, bear little relationship to the special problems of the foreign student. The latter must learn new speech rhythms and intonation patterns, acquire a more natural and less bookish delivery, form the habit of obscuring unstressed vowels, concentrate on unfamiliar sounds, and the like.

One or two especially fortunate institutions have been able to form entire classes made up of individuals with the same or very similar linguistic backgrounds. For these homogeneous groups very excellent teaching materials have been developed, based on a careful comparative study of the phonetic systems of English and the students' mother tongue. Such are the *Intensive Course in English for Latin American Students*, and the *Intensive Course in English for Chinese Students* of the University of Michigan's English Language Institute; and the *Syllabus for English Through Practice* (for speakers of Spanish) of Teachers College, Columbia University. These texts embody linguistic principles and utilize corrective techniques which seem to have a solid basis in scientific fact and which are in many cases new. They mark a long step forward in the teaching of American English as a second language.

Instructive as they may be to the average teacher of the subject, however, these and other similar texts still do not solve the problem of finding pronunciation materials for his own course. It is a regrettable but incontrovertible fact that the great majority of the classes in English for foreign students taught in the United States are and must continue to be composed of individuals from many different countries with many different first languages. The need in such courses is for materials adapted to the use of students with a wide variety of non-English linguistic backgrounds. Even in our cultural institutes abroad, texts with general applicability will certainly be needed for many years to come. It will be a long, long time before materials at all levels, dealing with all phases of instruction, for all major language groups, can be made available — if indeed we are ever to be so fortunate as to have them.

Introduction: to the Teacher

This *Manual of American English Pronunciation*, it is hoped, will go at least a little way toward filling the need. The text is definitely not for beginners. It is best suited to reasonably adult and literate students who have studied English several years back home or who have had some practical experience with the language in this country — the typical foreign student in an American college or university, the educated new immigrant, or the advanced student in a cultural institute.

It is based on the type of English known as General American, the language which may be heard, with only slight variations, from Ohio through the Middle West and on to the Pacific Coast. Some 90,000,000 people speak this General American. Living as they do in the region where the process of dialect mixing has gone farthest and where the language has achieved most uniformity, they undeniably constitute the present linguistic center of gravity of the English-speaking world, both because of their numbers and their cultural importance.

An attempt has been made to incorporate in the *Manual* many of the concepts and techniques developed by those who have applied the principles of linguistic science to English teaching. The British phoneticians have not been neglected as a source of ideas. The author has also drawn heavily upon the literature and practical classroom experience of our American modern foreign language teachers and speech correctionists. Throughout the text laboratory exercises are included, and suggestions are made as to how the instructor can strengthen his course by the use of various types of recording and play-back equipment.

The various parts of the *Manual* have been slowly developed,tested, revised in the classrooms of the University of California, Los Angeles, where English is a required subject for most newly entered students from other countries. Most of the materials have been tried out repeatedly over a period of several years by different instructors. Those enrolled in the classes came from all parts of the world, a cross section of our foreign student population. The chief linguistic groups represented were, in order: Spanish, Northern Chinese, Iranian, Arabic, Germanic, French, and Scandinavian. But there have been individuals from all the major language areas of the globe.

It has been the conviction of the instructional staff that, even though our pronunciation materials could not be based on a comparative study of the phonetics of English and one foreign language, they need not for that reason be completely unscientific. We felt that there were large categories of speech difficulties which all or many of our students had in common, and have found this in fact to be the case. Our first task was to discover as accurately and objectively as we could what these areas of common weakness were. A check list of categories was set up in accordance with the phonetic systems of several languages which have been more or less adequately described by scholars and which were known to us. We included, insofar as we could, all previously noted departures from the norms of the conversational pronunciation of educated native speakers of General American English. We then recorded the speech, analyzed and counted the "errors" of all our students for three years. The result was a sort of frequency count of the pronunciation difficulties of a group of several hundred average students from abroad. The *Manual* was built around this count.

We believe we have thus avoided two undesirable extremes: 1) a text organized solely in accordance with the subjective intuition of the author, and 2) one which logically and with equal emphasis treats all the elements of the English sound system without taking into consideration the special needs of the student group.

As the results of the frequency count became available, our next concern was to determine the order in which the various types of speech difficulty found to be prevalent in our mixed classes should be dealt with, and the relative amount of attention which should be devoted to each type. Our aim was to make the students' speech as completely intelligible as possible. Could this be best achieved by treating first and in most detail those difficulties which the count showed to be most common, by an arrangement based on simple numerical frequency? Or were there certain kinds of difficulty which were more serious than others, which affected intelligibility to a greater extent, and which consequently must be given greater emphasis?

We examined with considerable care the widely accepted assumption that "errors" involving the substitution of one phoneme[1] for another — pronouncing

---

1. Sound which may be the sole feature whereby one word is distinguished in meaning from another: for example, *time* [taɪm] and *dime* [daɪm] are alike except for their initial sounds; therefore [t] and [d] are phonemes in English.

that as [θæt] rather than [ðæt], or *bit* as [bit] instead of [bɪt] — are necessarily those which most affect intelligibility, and are consequently those which must always be attacked first. As we gained experience, we were more and more forced to the conclusion that, while this theory might have some validity with reference to beginning students, it was of little or no value as a guide in our advanced classes. Our count revealed that the substitution of one phoneme for another was relatively infrequent in the speech of our students. Only a few such substitutions — [ɪ] for [i], [ɪ] for [i], [ɔ] for [o], [a] for [ə], [s] for [z], [t] for [d], [d] for [ð], etc. — accounted for the great majority of cases. Most others, while theoretically possible or even likely, were actually quite uncommon and certainly could not be regarded as a problem of major importance. We found our students having almost no trouble with [m] or the diphthongs [aɪ], [aʊ] and [ɔɪ].

We were also impressed by the fact that in almost all cases of phonemic substitution, even in those where the mispronunciation should have resulted in giving the word a different meaning — *bit* as [bit] (beat) instead of [bɪt] —, the context made the intended meaning quite clear. In other words, the substitution seldom seemed to result in a misunderstanding. This impression was strengthened by the extreme difficulty we experienced in preparing drills made up of sentences in which either word of a minimal pair — *made-mate, time-dime, save-safe* — would be equally appropriate. Our students appeared simply to fail to understand a word much more often than they mistook it for some other word. We did not understand them a great deal more frequently than we misunderstood them.

On the other hand, certain non-phonemic "errors" proved in practice to be serious barriers to intelligibility, and were shown by our count to be extremely common. An Italian student had great difficulty in making himself understood because of his tendency to pronounce all final stops with a strong "finishing sound." For him and many others, the improper release and aspiration of stops was obviously a much more important problem than the substitution of, say, [ʃ] for [ʒ].

We found that a knowledge of voicing alone did not enable our students to make a clear distinction between words like *plays* [plez] and *place* [ples]. Better results were obtained when we also pointed out and drilled the so-called secondary differences between

[ez] and [es]: vowel length and consonant aspiration. These latter are not usually classified among the phonemic qualities of English sounds.

The author was recently struck by two very fine examples of how non-phonemic differences in sounds may even cause misunderstanding. With another American professor and several Filipino educational officials he was traveling by car near Manila to visit a school in the village of P̲olo, province of Bulak̲an. The other American asked one of the officials to repeat the name of our destination, and understood the answer to be B̲olo, Bulah̲an. [p] and [b], [k] and [h] all exist as separate phonemes in Tagalog, the native language of this particular Filipino. Initial [p] is unaspirated as well as unvoiced. In English, on the other hand, initial [p] is strongly aspirated, and initial [b] is not aspirated though it is voiced. The American, listening to a sentence in which the context gave him no clue, mistook the Filipino's unaspirated [p] for a [b]. We have traditionally regarded voicing or the lack of it as the feature which distinguishes the phoneme [p] from the phoneme [b]. But in this case aspiration was certainly the distinctive characteristic. The official had pronounced *Bulakan* with a perfectly normal Tagalog [k], formed far back in the throat with a very incomplete closure. In English this [k] would have been made farther toward the front of the mouth and with a strong closure. Though these latter qualities are not usually thought of as essential to the [k]-phoneme, their absence clearly made the American mistake [k] for [h].

When an individual begins the study of a foreign language, the new phonemes are often immediately obvious to him, and he therefore tends to learn them rather quickly. The American who takes up Tagalog cannot fail to become aware of the glottal stop [ʔ] which distinguishes a word like *bata* [bátaʔ] (child) from *bata* [báta] (gown). He will also, of necessity, learn very soon to use the phoneme [ŋ] at the beginning of a word, as in *ngalan* [ŋálan] (name), where it does not occur in English. But he may never notice or reproduce certain other features of the new sound system, such as the incomplete closure of [k] or the lack of aspiration of initial [p], unless these are pointed out to him. These latter are not obvious, though they may profoundly affect the ability of native speakers to understand the American's Tagalog.

We believe that any pronunciation text which devotes its attention almost exclusively to phonemic

Introduction: To the Teacher

differences concentrates on what is most obvious and most easily acquired through simple imitation. It neglects precisely those phases of the phonetics of the language in which imitation is most likely to fail, and analytical knowledge and systematic drill to be of greatest value.

Our own solution has been to regard unintelligibility not as the result of phonemic substitution, but as *the cumulative effect of many little departures from the phonetic norms of the language*. A great many of these departures may be phonemic; many others are not. Under certain circumstances, *any* abnormality of speech can contribute to unintelligibility.

This does not, of course, mean that we felt that we could dispense with the phoneme in the preparation of the *Manual*. The system of phonetic transcription adopted[2] is almost entirely phonemic, and the norms presented are phonemically defined, with Kenyon and Knott's *Pronouncing Dictionary of American English* as our authority. We make no attempt to treat such non-phonemic variants of sounds as would be natural in the language of a native speaker of English: e.g., the various regional and personal differences in the way the stressed vowel of *Mary* is pronounced. However, we do devote more attention than is usual to unnatural, "foreign sounding" variants, even though these may be non-phonemic.

The fact that any phonetic abnormality can contribute to unintelligibility does not mean, either, that all departures from the norm should be treated as

---

2. The symbols used for transcription in this text are those of the International Phonetic Alphabet adapted slightly for our particular purposes. In the interests of pedagogical simplicity we have used the single sign [ə] to represent the obscure vowels in the unstressed syllables of *alone* [əlón] and *after* [æftər] as well as the stressed vowels of *cut* [kət] and *bird* [bərd]. To transcribe the initial sound of *you* [yu], [y] was preferred to [j], since the latter symbol very strongly suggests certain other sounds to speakers of Spanish, French, etc. [hw] has proved easier to teach than [ʍ]: *white* [hwaɪt]. The "centering" diphthongs, [iə], [ɪə], [eə], [ɛə], and [æə], were included among our symbols as a graphic means of representing the peculiar quality possessed by a front vowel when it stands before [l] or [r]; we have found the transcription of *will* as [wɪəl] a very definite aid in avoiding "clear" [l]'s. We have also departed from custom in placing the accent marks which indicate stressed syllables over the vowel of the syllable: *taken* [tékən]; perhaps because of the influence of their native orthography, many of our students seem to recognize marks in this position more readily than they do accents placed at the beginning of the syllable.

though they were of equal importance. We have adopted an order of arrangement based primarily on simple numerical frequency, considering first and at greatest length those difficulties most prevalent in our classes. It was necessary at times, of course, to modify this arrangement, in the interests of logic and good pedagogy, by grouping similar problems together. We also considered that an "error" which involved an entire sentence, such as a faulty intonation pattern, was obviously of more importance than one which affected only a single sound.

Problems such as improper voicing, aspiration, and vowel length, which recur in connection with a series of different consonants or vowels, we have treated as a whole rather than as matters to be taken up over and over again in connection with each individual sound. In other words, we felt that the substitution of [k] for its voiced counterpart [g] in a word like *big* [bɪg] reflected not so much an imperfect control of these two sounds as it did a general inability to voice final consonants. We noted that students who substituted [bɪk] for *big* [bɪg] also almost invariably substituted [etʃ] for *age* [edʒ] and [ɪs] for *is* [ɪz]. We consequently did not prepare a separate section and drills on [k] and [g], but included these sounds in a lesson on voicing. For the same reason we did not attempt to drill all difficult consonant clusters separately, but treated the problem they represent in sections on blending, consonant combinations, and the prothetic s. In a sense, then, our approach has been synthetic rather than analytical.

In its final form the *Manual* has a cyclic arrangement. After an initial lesson which introduces the student to the symbols of the International Phonetic Alphabet, it procedes at once to the problem of the obscuring of unstressed vowels, explaining only enough about vowel classification to make the significance of obscuration and the identity of the vowel sounds clear. It then moves on to the closely related and crucially important subject of rhythm and stress in words and sentences. The elements of intonation and the connection between intonation patterns and stress are next treated in two lessons. Until some control of rhythm and intonation have been achieved, drills involving connected discourse may do more harm than good, and it is futile to hope to achieve mastery of the individual sounds which make up the larger patterns. If the pattern is wrong, the sounds cannot be entirely correct. If the pattern is right, correct sounds are much easier to produce.

In Lessons VII and VIII the principles of conso-

Introduction: To the Teacher xvii

nant classification, voicing, and aspiration are explained and applied, with particular emphasis on the pronunciation of the endings -s and -ed, and the effect of an initial or final position on articulation. Lesson IX deals with the glides [l] and [r], their influence on preceding vowel sounds, and also with the group of syllabic consonants.

Attention is then shifted back to vowels. Detailed analyses of the formation of the individual sounds are given, and the problem of tonic vowel substitutions is attacked. Substitutions caused by defective articulation are first considered, then those which result from the inconsistencies of English spelling and from the influence of the orthography of the student's native language.

The last two lessons of the *Manual* deal with prevalent consonant substitutions which are the effect, not of improper voicing or aspiration, but of a formation of the individual sounds which is faulty in some other respect

II. Use of the Manual.

Since the *Manual* is not intended for beginners, but for individuals who have already read a great deal of English and are familiar with the traditional orthography of common words, there seemed to be no advantage in writing all exercises in phonetic symbols in an attempt to guard the students against spelling-pronunciations. A great deal of transcribed material with intonation and stress markings has been included, however, especially in the earlier lessons. The purpose of these transcriptions is to facilitate the breaking up of old speech habits by providing a new type of visual stimulus, to make it possible for the student's analytical faculties to intervene more effectively in the formation of sounds and patterns of sound. This effect is best achieved as he first becomes familiar with symbols, and the law of diminishing returns appears to make itself felt soon thereafter. Toward the end of the text special symbols and markings are used more and more sparingly, and the transition is thus made back to normal orthography, to the language situation in which the student has been finding himself all along in his other classes and in which he will continue to use English.

It was never intended that the *Manual* should teach students to make phonetic transcriptions and to mark intonation themselves. All that is aimed at is an ability to read symbols and to follow intonation lines. It is true that in several cases the class is asked to transcribe and mark the intonation patterns of a few carefully chosen sentences. The purpose of these exercises, however, is merely to achieve passive recognition more rapidly by means of a little active experience. The instructor is strongly warned against making the ability to write in phonetic symbols an end in itself.

Whenever possible, the exercises provided are made up of entire sentences and even connected paragraphs rather than of individual words. A simple vocabulary chosen from Thorndike's first few hundred words has been used, and the subject matter has been drawn largely from the situations of everyday life most familiar to the students. There are no special review lessons, but every lesson contains review exercises; great care has been taken to insure the recall of important principles at spaced intervals.

Even so, it is recognized that any course in English pronunciation which asked of its students no more than the completion of the work prescribed in the pages of this *Manual* would be woefully incomplete. Analytical explanations and controlled drills such as those of the text certainly are a necessary part of a pronunciation course; there seems to be no other way to break up deeply ingrained habits of faulty speech and to initiate the formation of new habits. But the best way to learn pronunciation is by pronouncing. There is no substitute for extensive imitation and practice under conditions as nearly approaching those of everyday life as is possible. No textbook, no amount of analytical work can fully supply this need.

It is therefore hoped that the instructor will supplement the work of the text in various ways. He should encourage his students to carry on outside of class the oral reading suggested at the end of almost every lesson, and himself find opportunities for urging that even more such reading be done. Better integration will be secured if the materials read are those used in other phases of the student's work in English, or in his classes in other subjects. That is why relatively few readings have been included in the *Manual* itself. During reading practice, the student's attention should be focused on one type of difficulty: for example, final -*ed*, or the stress of compound words. This will give purpose and direction to his reading, and perhaps enable him to progress from the point at which he can avoid a given "error" by consious effort

Introduction: To the Teacher

to the point where he makes the correct sound automatically when he is thinking only of the meaning of his words.

With the same end in view, we have done quite a bit of play-reading in our classes at the University of California. Using such props as the classroom can afford, books in hand, the students read the lines and walk through the actions. In selecting plays, we give preference to those which are written in a simple, modern, conversational language free from dialectal peculiarities. A large cast and well distributed lines are also advantages, as they make it possible for more individuals to participate. We have found Thornton Wilder's *Our Town* and Kaufman and Hart's *You Can't Take it With You* to be quite suitable. While the play is going on, coaching from the instructor is kept at an absolute minimum, but the attention of the participants is focused on some particular speech problem. Sometimes the text is prepared in advance by marking all words in which the particular problem occurs: for example, all final s's.

The supplementary practice may also take the form of reading by the instructor and direct imitation on the part of the students.

It should be kept in mind, however, that most language is not read, but is in the form of free conversation, for which an exclusive diet of reading is inadequate preparation. In several of the lessons devices are suggested whereby the instructor can get his students to carry on a more or less spontaneous conversation, while he listens to hear that they produce certain sounds or patterns correctly. It is hoped that time will be found in the class for many more such exercises. Rising intonation could be practiced by asking members of the group to question one another about their plans for the future. Syllabic consonants could be drilled by writing on the blackboard a list of words containing such sounds, and asking the students to tell if any of these words have interesting associations for them. This kind of work fixes attention on thought content rather than sound production. If skillfully carried out, it can have great value as a means of progressing gradually from the conscious to the unconscious control of a feature of pronunciation, as a way of adding one more analyzed element to the synthesis of normal speech.

How much time would be required for completion of the *Manual* within the framework of a course such as is here described? Ideally, three instructional hours per week for two semesters, a total of approximately ninety hours, would not be excessive. The entire program — text, laboratory work with recording equipment, supplementary reading and conversational practice — could be effectively developed within a course of those dimensions. Unfortunately, that much time will often not be available, especially if pronunciation is to be taught only as one phase of a general course in English for foreign students.

If forced to eliminate items from the program, the author would probably first omit Lessons XII and XIII of the *Manual*, which deal with the relationship between the traditional spelling and the pronunciation of words. Vital as laboratory work is, it is also very time consuming, and a great deal of it simply cannot be carried out in a short course. The teacher may find throughout the text an occasional long exercise which, in case of necessity, can be passed up. Lessons I through IX constitute, in our opinion, the hard core of the book. With a small, well prepared group, some practical results might be achieved in as little as thirty hours of class time.

III. Use of the Accent Inventory.

The *Accent Inventory* of the *Manual* should be of service in a wide variety of ways to resourceful teachers. Here we can only suggest some of the fundamental and particularly effective uses to which it may be put, as shown by actual classroom experience.

As its name suggests, the basic function of the *Inventory* is to make it possible to take stock of the types of difficulty each student is having with English speech at the beginning of the semester's or year's work. It provides a diagnosis of individual weaknesses and a prescription of corrective measures. It should also facilitate the teacher's task of deciding which sections of the *Manual* are to be stressed in work with the entire class.

The *Diagnostic Passage* is recorded in permanent form by each student as early in the course as possible. This passage, on which the *Inventory* is based, is only eight sentences long. Admittedly, somewhat more revealing results might be achieved if the analysis could be based on a large volume of spontaneous conversational material, rather than on a few sentences to be read. Students do get tense when they know they are being tested, and the intonations of oral reading may often vary from those of ordinary conversation. The

Introduction: To the Teacher xxi

conversation-based inventory, however, because of the tremendous amount of time and ingenuity it requires, can hardly be carried out effectively and systematically with an entire class. The reading of the eight sentences is a practical substitute, which will be valid to the extent that the teacher succeeds in putting each student at his ease when the recording is made, and getting him to read naturally and informally. The sentences should be treated, so far as possible, as a matter-of-fact conversation, involving no unusual emotion or stresses.

Based as it is on the reading of a very small amount of material, the *Inventory* can probably be well carried out only if the *Diagnostic Passage* is recorded. No teacher's ear and hand would be quick enough to note all the elements of faulty diction while listening to a single reading of so brief a passage. And repeated readings always vary slightly. A record, on the other hand, may be taken home and played any number of times as the diagnostician jots down what he hears.

The student is requested to make this initial recording with nothing more in the way of preparation than a casual preliminary reading of the *Diagnostic Passage* at home to familiarize himself with the thought of the sentences. If the teacher will record his own "correct" version of each sentence immediately after the student's version, the subsequent usefulness of the recording will be increased.

The teacher then analyzes the students' version of the eight sentences. The *Inventory* is printed as a separate booklet so that the copy of each member of the class may be taken up and kept while this process is going on. The teacher plays each recording repeatedly and makes notes of "errors" heard until he feels his analysis is reasonably complete. The various classifications of the *Inventory* should help the inexperienced diagnostician listen systematically and recognize some elements of the foreign "accent" which he or she might not otherwise have noticed. For this analytical work, a play-back machine with a foot pedal by means of which the pick-up arm can be controlled automatically is extremely useful. With such a pedal, the machine may be stopped and started instantaneously without tone distortion, and be made to repeat sentences and even words. Equipment of this type is on the market and not particularly expensive. For note taking, and as an office record, the teacher may find it convenient to have on hand a supply of mimeographed copies of the *Diagnostic Passage*.

When he has made adequate notes, the teacher corrects the *Diagnostic Passage* and fills out the blanks of the *Inventory* proper in each student's booklet. Detailed suggestions for doing this will be found in the booklet itself.

In the first column of the *Inventory* pages the diagnostician should merely check the general types of "error" he notes. In column two specific "errors" should be marked and, whenever possible, the nature of the mistake should be shown — both what the student said and what he should have said. It is well to use only the broad symbols which are explained in the *Manual* and which the student may therefore be expected eventually to understand: e.g., in case *it* is pronounced with a vowel between [i] and [ɪ], use the [i] symbol in marking the error.

In phrases like *let me* (Sentence 1), if the t is merely pronounced with too much aspiration, the error is classified under Section IV-E of the *Inventory*; on the other hand, if the student goes so far in his efforts to pronounce t clearly as to insert an [ə] between t and m in addition to aspirating the t and thus disturbs the rhythm of the sentence, the error is classified under I-D-1. Most errors in the voicing of consonants are classified under IV-A, but the substitution of [t] for [d] and [s] for [z] in the endings -ed and -s is found under V-A and B. Because of the arrangement of the *Manual* and the fact that errors in the pronunciation of -ed and -s may involve vowels as well as consonants, it seemed best to make separate headings in the *Inventory* (V-A and B) to cover errors of choice between [d] - [t] - [ɪd] and [z] - [s] - [ɪz]. If -ed or -s is omitted altogether, the error should be noted under IV-H-2-5. In the case of errors involving a front vowel before [l] or [r], as in *feel* (Sentence 7), the substitution of [fɪəl] for [fiəl] should be classified under III-D, but the substitution of [fil] for [fiəl] should be noted under V-D.

The corrected and marked copies of the *Inventory* booklets are not returned to the students until the latter have completed their study of at least the first four or five lessons of the *Manual*, and can therefore be expected to recognize most of the symbols used and understand something of the principles involved. At the time the booklets are returned, every effort should be made to impress on the class the significance of this diagnosis and prescription. It should be pointed out that each heading of the *Inventory* contains a reference to the section of the *Manual* in which that particular type of speech difficulty is treated. The booklet will serve as an individual guide to the text. Every member of the class should study his own weaknesses carefully. He should mark in some way those sections of the *Manual* which are of particular concern to him, and which he should review or concentrate his future attention on.

When the student has had time to study his diagnosis, he is given an opportunity individually or in class to listen as his recording is played. The purpose of this is to permit him to "hear his own mistakes," a very necessary first step in accent correction. Clear realization of shortcomings must precede improvement. As he listens to himself, the student should have before his eyes the corrected *Diagnostic Passage* in his booklet.

The class will have many occasions for extensive pronunciation work of various kinds in the fifteen lessons which make up the body of the *Manual*, and in the additional oral reading and conversation which may be suggested by the instructor. The *Inventory*, on the other hand, can be used to motivate complementary intensive exercise -- frequently repeated drills concentrated on a very small amount of material with absolute mastery as the aim in view. If a student could succeed in learning to repeat just the eight sentences of the *Diagnostic Passage* perfectly, without trace of "accent," it would mean that he had probably acquired sufficient control over his organs of speech to enable him eventually to correct all his faulty speech habits. Perfection in these eight sentences may then be urged on the class as one of the specific objectives of the course.

The drills aimed at the achievement of such mastery may take various forms. The student should certainly repeat the eight sentences as often as possible. In his laboratory period he may play his recording frequently, and try to imitate the teacher's "correct" version of each sentence. A particularly effective type of intensive drill may be carried out if there is available a play-back machine with a foot pedal which controls its pick-up arm -- the mechanism mentioned in a preceding paragraph. By means of this pedal, the machine can be made to repeat each of the teachers "correct" sentences many times at quick, regular intervals. The student first listens, then imitates again and again, paying particular attention to timing, intonation, and the grouping of words. When the teacher thinks the imitation is rather good, he stops the machine and lets the student repeat two or three times more in the same rhythm, without the accompaniment of the recorded voice.

New recordings of the *Diagnostic Passage* may, of course, be made at any time during the term. A last recording and quick analysis, carried out as part of the final examination, will help the teacher assign grades based on objective evidence of practical achievement. This chance to hear himself again at the end of the course, and to compare his speech at that time with his earliest efforts, should send the conscientious student away from the class with a most gratifying realization of the progress he has made.

LESSON I

The Phonetic Alphabet

I. Learning to Pronounce English.

The fundamental method by which a student learns to pronounce English is by imitating the pronunciation of English-speaking persons. During this course you will have many opportunities to imitate the speech of your instructor and others; do so as accurately and as often as you can. The strange new sounds and rhythms may seem a little funny at first, but you must try to forget that, and imitate without reservations. You have probably been amused at the peculiarities in the speech of an American pronouncing, or attempting to pronounce, your own language; now you must try to reproduce those same peculiarities in English. Your success will depend largely on the sharpness of your ear and your ability as an imitator.

Sometimes imitation does fail, however. The instructor may pronounce a word many times for you, and you still may be unable to say it exactly as he does. This may be because you are hearing and reproducing well only a few of the most important sounds which make up the word. It will be of benefit to you then if the instructor can write out the word for you, sound by sound, using symbols which are always pronounced in the same way. One of the most typical features of English is the manner in which its unimportant, unstressed vowels are pronounced. Your attention may not be called to these at all when you *hear* a word spoken, but you can *see* them as clearly as the stressed vowels in a phonetic transcription. The eye is more analytical than the ear. We can see separately all the symbols which make up a written word, but we can hardly hear individually all the sounds which compose it as it is normally spoken.

Most people learn most things better through the

eye than through the ear. Even in learning to pronounce, where you must depend primarily on hearing, there is every advantage in being able to have your eye aid your ear. Something learned in two different ways is probably four times as well learned. The ordinary spelling of an English word has so little relation to its sound that the former is nearly useless as a guide to pronunciation.

There will be times when you may wish to write down the pronunciation of a new word, so as to be able to recall it later. Unfortunately, we cannot remember a mere sound clearly for very long; but a phonetic transcription will make recall easier. When there is no English-speaking person present to pronounce a word for you, your only recourse may be to try to reconstruct the sound of the word from the symbols in a dictionary. Practice in reading symbols will help you learn to make accurate reconstructions.

There will be times too when, to succeed in making an English sound perfectly, you will need to know exactly what to do with your tongue, lips, and other organs of speech. For instance, in order to make the t-sound in English the tip of the tongue touches the roof of the mouth somewhat farther back than is the case with most other languages. Merely hearing the t and trying to imitate it, you might never guess this fact.

In other words, though you must rely chiefly on your ear and imitation to acquire a good accent, a knowledge of the number and identity of English sounds, the symbols used to represent them in phonetic writing, the way in which they are produced, and a few of the laws that govern their behavior will be of great advantage to you and will increase your chances of success. This text is designed to give you such information and to aid you in learning to apply it. The text is not a course in English pronunciation, but merely a useful aid in such a course. The science of phonetics may be considered the grammar of pronunciation: a knowledge of phonetics will help you to pronounce no less, and no more, than a knowledge of grammar will teach you to speak and write.

II. Why the International Phonetic Alphabet?

The first step in your work with phonetics will be to familiarize yourself with a set of symbols by means of which the important sounds of English — all those which serve to distinguish one word from another word[1] — may be represented. There must be a symbol for every such sound, and no more than one symbol for any given sound.

The system we shall use is a version of that known as the International Phonetic Alphabet. Because of its small number of vowel symbols, one for each of the eleven fundamental English vowels, it is better suited to our purpose than such systems of diacritical markings as those employed in some of our well-known dictionaries. Use of the latter may involve learning some thirty different vowel symbols, with each sound represented by several different symbols.

Besides, the International Phonetic Alphabet, or I.P.A., has the advantage of being more widely known than any other system. It was developed through the cooperative efforts of some of the world's leading linguistic scholars, and is almost universally used today in serious works on pronunciation, in speech courses, pronouncing dictionaries, elementary French texts in the United States, English texts in Argentina and Chile, and so on.

You will find I.P.A. symbols in several of the important dictionaries you may wish to refer to and perhaps own: Kenyon and Knott, *A Pronouncing Dictionary of American English*[2], D. Jones, *An English Pronouncing Dictionary*, Cassell's *New French Dictionary* (French-English, English-French), Cassell's *New German Dictionary* (German-English, English-German), Heath's *New German Dictionary*, Heath's *Standard French and English Dictionary*, Kenkyusha's *New English-Japanese Dictionary*, etc. *The American College Dictionary*, which is perhaps the best of our recently published all-English dictionaries for general university use, employs a set of symbols which represents a compromise between

---

1. Recognition of the difference between *bed* and *bead*, when the words are spoken, depends on ability to distinguish between the vowel sounds in the two words. There must, therefore, be separate symbols to represent these two sounds. The r̩ in the word *water* is pronounced in different ways in various parts of the United States and Great Britain, but variety of pronunciation does not mean variety of meaning. For our purposes, one symbol will suffice to represent the various r̩ sounds. An alphabet based on this principle is properly called a phonemic alphabet. The version of the International Phonetic Alphabet used in this text is phonemic, except that, for pedagogical reasons, we have introduced the diphthong symbols [æə], [ɛə], [eə], [ɪə], [iə] to represent certain types of vowels followed by l̩ and r̩.

2. Springfield, G. and C. Merriam Co., 1944, $3.00. This is by all odds the best pronouncing dictionary of American English, and a foreign student of the language will find it an invaluable tool. Note, however, that it gives only the pronunciation of a word, not its meaning, derivation, and the like.

the Webster diacritical markings and the I.P.A.

III. Table of Symbols.

In the table which follows are included approximate French, German, and Spanish equivalents for most of the American English sounds. These equivalents are not scientifically accurate in most cases, and are given only because they may make it easier at first for you to identify the various sounds.

A written accent marks the stressed vowel of words of more than one syllable: kodak [kódæk]. In case there are two or more stressed syllables, the most important is marked [´], and that with secondary stress [˝]: preposition [prɛ̋pəzíʃən].

The International Phonetic Alphabet

Symbol	English Examples	Approximate Equivalent in:		
		French	German	Spanish

Consonants:

1.	b	boat [bot]	bébé	baden	también
2.	d	dark [dark]	doigt	dumm	un dedo
3.	f	far [far]	fait	Feind	fino
4.	g	gold [gold]	garder	gut	golpe
5.	h	home [hom]	(none)	haben	gente
6.	k	cold [kold] kodak [kódæk]	car	kaufen	vaca
7.	l	let [lɛt]	laisser	lange	lado
8.	m	man [mæn]	même	morgen	mano
9.	n	next [nɛkst]	non	nein	nombre
10.	ŋ	ring [rɪŋ] sink [sɪŋk]	(none)	singen	naranja
11.	p	part [part]	peu	Papier	pelo
12.	r	rest [rɛst]	(none)	(none)	(none)
13.	s	send [sɛnd] city [sɪtɪ]	sou	Haus	sino
14.	ʃ	ship [ʃɪp]	chez	schön	(none)
15.	t	ten [tɛn]	temps	Tür	tener
16.	θ	think [θɪŋk]	(none)	(none)	cita (as pronounced in Madrid)
17.	ð	that [ðæt]	(none)	(none)	dedo
18.	v	very [vɛrɪ]	vain	November	(none)
19.	w	went [wɛnt]	oui	(none)	huevo
20.	y	you [yu]	hier	jung	bien
21.	z	zoo [zu] rose [roz] knows [noz]	chose	dieser	mismo

American English Pronunciation   5

The International Phonetic Alphabet

Symbol	English Examples	Approximate Equivalent in:		
		French	German	Spanish
22. ʒ	plea_s_ure [plɛ́ʒər] vi_s_ion [vɪ́ʒən]	_j_e	(none)	(none)
23. hw	_wh_en [hwɛn]	(none)	(none)	(none)
24. tʃ	_ch_ildren [tʃɪ́ldrən]	t_ch_èque	Put_sch_	mu_ch_o
25. dʒ	_j_ury [dʒúrɪ] e_dge_ [ɛdʒ] a_ge_ [edʒ]	_dj_inn	(none)	_y_o (as pronounced in Argentina)

Vowels:

1. ɑ	f_a_r [fɑr] h_o_t [hɑt]	â_m_e	V_a_ter	m_a_lo
2. æ	_a_m [æm]	m_a_l	(none)	(none)
3. e	l_a_te [let] r_ai_se [rez]	th_é_	L_e_ben	p_ei_ne
4. ɛ	g_e_t [gɛt] br_ea_d [brɛd] s_ai_d [sɛd]	l_è_ve	B_e_tt	_e_l
5. i	s_ee_ [si] rec_ei_ve [rɪsív] r_ea_ch [ritʃ]	f_i_ni	s_ie_ht	m_i_sa
6. ɪ	_i_n [ɪn] b_e_come [bɪkə́m]	(none)	s_i_tzen	(none)
7. ɔ	f_o_r [fɔr] _a_ll [ɔl] _ou_ght [ɔt]	n_o_te	w_o_llen	_o_rden
8. o	g_o_ [go] c_oa_t [kot]	dô_m_e	B_oo_t	b_ou_
9. u	r_u_le [rul] t_oo_ [tu]	f_ou_	St_u_be	m_u_la
10. ʊ	p_u_t [pʊt] c_ou_ld [kʊd] g_oo_d [gʊd]	(none)	d_u_nkel	(none)
11. ə	b_u_t [bət] b_i_rd [bərd] _o_th_er_ [ə́ðər] _a_go [əgó] r_ea_s_o_n [rízən]	m_e_	Knab_e_	(none)

| Symbol | English | French | German | Spanish |

Diphthongs³ (combinations of two vowel sounds):

1. aɪ   I [aɪ]   aïe   mein   hay
         cry [kraɪ]
2. aʊ   now [naʊ]   (none)   Haupt   pausa
         house [haʊs]
3. æə   shall [ʃæəl]   (none)   (none)   (none)
4. ɛə   well [wɛəl]   plaie (as   (none)   (none)
         there   pronounced in
         [ðɛər]   the Midi)
5. eə   sale [seəl]   née (as pro-   (none)   (none)
         mayor   nounced in
         [meər]   the Midi)
6. iə   feel [fiəl]   vie (as pro-   (none)   (none)
         we're [wiər]   nounced in
                          the Midi)
7. ɪə   hill [hɪəl]   (none)   (none)   (none)
         hear [hɪər]
8. ɔɪ   boy [bɔɪ]   (none)   heute   sois
         noise [nɔɪz]

Various phonetic markings:

1. ʔ   Indicates a glottal stop: *oh, oh* [oʔo], as in "Oh, oh! Look what I did" (see Lesson IV, Section IV).
2. ʰ   Means that the preceding consonant sound is strongly aspirated: *time* [tʰaɪm] (see Lesson VIII, Section I).
3. ː   Means that the preceding sound is lengthened: the [i] of *bead* biːd is longer than the [i] of *beat* [bit] (see Lesson VIII, Section II).
4. ˌ   Means that the consonant under which it is placed is pronounced as a syllabic: *didn't* [dɪdn̩t], *little* [lɪtl̩] (see Lesson IX, Section III).

IV. How Words are Transcribed.

Note that the I.P.A. symbols should be printed

---

3. By some phoneticians the vowels [e], as in *late* [let], and [o], as in *coat* [kot], are written as diphthongs: [eɪ] and [oʊ]. There is no doubt that both vowels really are diphthongs, as are almost all the other vowel sounds in English. However, the diphthongization of [e] and [o] is much more noticeable in certain varieties of British speech than in Standard American English. For the sake of simplicity and practicality, [e] and [o] are written in this text with a single symbol. The combinations [yu], in *few* [fyu], *uniform* [yunɪfɔrm]; [yə] in *young* [yəŋ], *figure* [fɪgyər]; [wi] in *weep* [wip]; [wɛ] in *west* [wɛst]; etc., could also be classified as diphthongs, but are considered in this *Manual* as consonant-vowel combinations rather than combinations of two vowels.

rather than written cursively, so that they may more
easily be read. In order that words spelled out in the
traditional manner may not be confused with phonetic
transcriptions, the latter should always be enclosed in
square brackets: *fish* is pronounced as [fɪʃ].

In transcribing a word in phonetic symbols, the
guiding principle to be kept in mind is that the transcription must represent *all* the distinctive sounds
heard when the word is pronounced, and *only* those
sounds. Do not be misled by the traditional spelling.
Silent letters -- those not heard in the pronunciation
of the word -- are not transcribed: eg., the e in *bone*
[bon], and the gh in *eight* [et]. Doubled consonants
usually do not mean that the consonant is pronounced
twice, so they are replaced in transcriptions by single
consonants: *matter* [mætər]. Two words may be spelled
differently, as are *sun* and *son*, but pronounced and
transcribed alike: [sən]. On the other hand, if a word
has two or more different pronunciations when used in
different ways, as has *bow*, these must be represented
by different transcriptions: [baʊ], "to bend one's
head"; and [bo], "instrument used for shooting arrows".

As has been pointed out, the I.P.A. provides a
symbol, but only one symbol, for each distinctive English sound. A great many of these symbols -- [b], [d],
[f], [k], [l], [m], [n], [p], [r], [t], [v], [w], and
[z] -- are exactly like the normal printed letters of
the alphabet; as symbols they *always* represent the same
sound which they *usually* represent as letters. These
are, of course, very easy to remember. Certain other
symbols are also just like normal letters; but the symbol always has the same sound, whereas the corresponding letter is commonly pronounced in more than one way:

    [g] always like the g in *good* [gʊd]
        never like the g in *George* [dʒordʒ]
    [s] always like the s in *said* [sɛd]
        never like the s in *rise* [raɪz]
    [h] always pronounced as in *home* [hom]
        never silent as in *hour* [aʊr]
    [y] always a consonant as in *you* [yu]
        never a vowel as in *city* [sɪtɪ]

For some other sounds, the traditional letters
cannot serve as symbols, and it is necessary to provide
new symbols. Since these may be strange to you, to
learn them well will require a special effort. Most
vowel symbols fall in this class. The eleven vowel
sounds of English cannot be represented accurately and
simply by the five letters normally used in spelling
vowels. Lesson II will help you to associate the

eleven vowel symbols of our version of the I.P.A. with the eleven sounds they represent. The new consonant symbol [ŋ] is necessary because the spelling ng is confusing. In words spelled with ng the g is usually silent, as in ring [rɪŋ]; we could not represent ring in symbols as [rɪng], since no phonetic symbol is silent, and the [n]-symbol must always have the same sound. In the same way we need [ʃ], which usually represents the letters sh, because the sh-sound cannot be made by simply pronouncing [s] and then [h]. [ʒ], as in vision [vɪʒən], is a rather rare English sound, spelled with letters which are ordinarily pronounced in quite a different way in other words. The [θ] and [ð]-symbols are needed, because the two distinctive sounds they represent are normally both written in the same way, with the letters th: thigh [θaɪ], thy [ðaɪ].

Not all of the letters which represent consonants in English are needed as phonetic symbols. Thus the letter c is usually pronounced like an s or a k, and is transcribed as [s] or [k]: city [sɪtɪ] cool [kul]. C is therefore not used as a symbol in transcriptions. For similar reasons, the letters j, q, and x are not used as symbols. To represent j we have the [dʒ] which is also used in transcribing the "soft" sound of g: just [dʒəst], age [edʒ]. The combination qu is transcribed as [kw]: quick [kwɪk]. X is usually transcribed as [ks] or [gz]: fix [fɪks], exact [ɪgzækt].

V. Exercises

A. Go through the Table several times, pronouncing the sound represented by each symbol.

B. Pronounce:

1. m	8. ʊ	15. ʒ	22. z	29. aʊ
2. æ	9. dʒ	16. o	23. ɪə	30. ð
3. ʃ	10. g	17. ɔ	24. ɔɪ	31. æə
4. ɛ	11. u	18. ŋ	25. θ	32. b
5. i	12. ə	19. e	26. v	
6. ɪ	13. y	20. tʃ	27. w	
7. hw	14. a	21. s	28. aɪ	

C. Pronounce these combinations of sounds:

1. pa	6. aʊdʒ	11. θɔɪ	16. aɪm	21. ðe
2. tʃo	7. hwi	12. ɪd	17. yo	22. yə
3. ez	8. ɪər	13. gæ	18. ɔk	23. æg
4. wɔ	9. ʊŋ	14. dʒə	19. av	24. θɪ
5. ðu	10. ɛn	15. ʃɛ	20. ɪŋ	25. æəl

D. Pronounce these very common words and write them as they are usually spelled in English:

1. tɚn   6. sɪŋ   11. traɪ   16. hu   21. mǽtɚ
2. ɜɪks 7. dʒəst   12. kɔz   17. hwɪtʃ   22. rézɪz
3. læst 8. θri   13. tɑp   18. smɔl   23. rízən
4. kʊd   9. taʊn   14. ðɛm   19. ðo   24. pléʒɚ
5. bɔɪz 10. gɑd   15. hɪər   20. yəŋ   25. mə́nɪ

E. Can you read these phrases?
   1. ɪnðəmɔ́rnɪŋ   4. əvðətítʃər
   2. ənɪ́ŋlɪʃklǽs   5. ɪnəmɪ́nɪt
   3. wɪərglǽd

LESSON II

Classification of Vowels

I. The Five Fundamental Vowels.

The fundamental vowel sounds, those which occur in almost all languages, are [a], [e], [i], [o], and [u]. It is worth noting that, with the exception of [a], the symbols for these five sounds are normal roman letters. The relationships of the five to one another may be shown graphically by means of a device known as the Viëtor triangle.

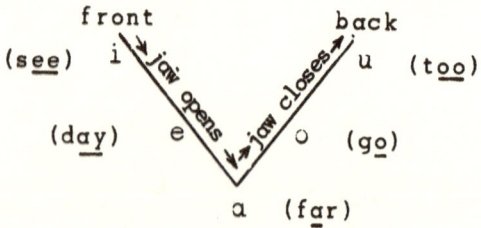

The vowel pronounced farthest to the front of the mouth is [i]. Pronounce that sound; then pronounce [e]. In moving from [i] to [e], note that there are two important changes in the position of the organs of speech: the jaw is lowered, and the spot where the tongue approaches the roof of the mouth most closely is shifted away from the front teeth toward the throat. If you pronounce [e], then [a], you will feel the same two types of change occur again. From [a] to [o], the movement from front to back continues, but the jaw begins to rise, or close, again; and these two movements also mark the shift from [o] to [u].

Now pronounce several times the entire series [i-e-a-o-u], and try to feel the regular progression in the organs of speech: from front to back, as you move from

American English Pronunciation

left to right on the triangle; and with jaw lower, then higher again, as you move from top to bottom, then back to the top, of the triangle. Note also that the lips are widely spread for [i], that the amount of spreading decreases with [e] and [a], and that the lips are rounded for [o] and [u].

The drawing below may help you to understand how different positions of the tongue correspond to different parts of the triangle.

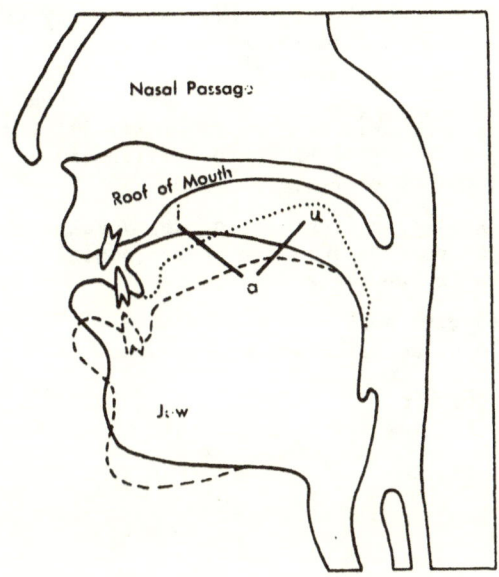

Tongue Position for [i], [a], and [u]

II. The Eleven Vowels of American English.

Students of English are usually well acquainted with the five fundamental vowel sounds, and find them quite easy to pronounce and identify. Familiarity with them may help you to master the six other vowels in the language, those which are represented by symbols unlike those of the ordinary roman alphabet: [I], [ɛ], [æ], [ɔ], [ʊ], and [ə].

[I] represents a sound intermediate between [i] and [e]. In other words, [I] is farther back than [i], but farther forward than [e]; pronounced with the jaw and tongue lower than [i], but higher than [e]. This relationship should be obvious to you if you will repeat three or four times the series [i-ɪ-e].

Between [e] and [a] there are two intermediate vowels: first [ɛ], then, a little farther back and lower, [æ].

Between [a] and [o] is [ɔ], and between [o] and [u] is [ʊ].

This leaves only the position of [ə] to be determined. It may be called the lazy man's vowel, since it is the sound a person produces when his speech organs are relaxed and in a neutral position. It is the sound you make when you do not quite know what you are going to say and are looking for the right words: "It's not that. Uh-h-h ... How shall I say it? Uh-h-h ..." For reasons that will be explained in the next lesson, [ə] is also the most frequently heard of all the English vowels; you will need to recognize it and make it about as often as [i], [e], [ɛ], [æ], [a], [ɔ], [o], [ʊ], and [u] combined. [ə] is the typical vowel which, more than any other sound, distinguishes English from the other languages of Western Europe.

Since it is neither a front nor a back vowel, neither as close as [i] nor as open as [a], its proper position on the Viëtor triangle is in the center.

The triangle, with each of the eleven vowels of American English in its place, would appear as follows:

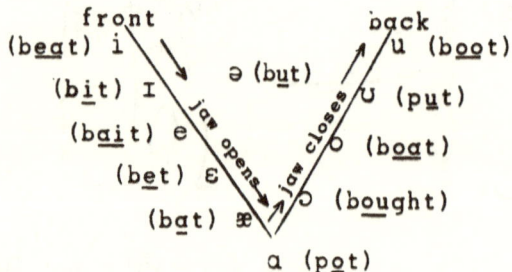

When a student of English mispronounces the vowel in a word, what he usually does is to substitute for the correct sound another sound very close to it. In other words, if you mispronounce the [ɪ] of bit, you will probably say beat [bit]. [ɔ] is usually confused with either [a] or [o], the sounds which appear on either side of it in the diagram. [æ] is confused with [ɛ] and [a]; [ɛ] with [e] and [æ], etc., etc. [ə], because of the position of the speech organs when it is made, may easily be mistaken for any of the other ten vowel sounds.

Notice that a word containing the sound appears in parentheses beside each symbol on the diagram. The only difference between the pronunciation of boot and but is the difference between [u] and [ə]. That is to say, the very meaning of the word

American English Pronunciation

depends on the quality of the vowel. If you wish to understand and be understood in English, you must be able to distinguish and make the distinction between the vowel sounds with absolute accuracy.

III. Exercises.

A. Pronounce the ten vowel sounds around the edges of the triangle several times in order, beginning first with [i], then with [u], and note carefully how the speech organs move in a regular progression as you pass from one symbol to another.

B. Learn to draw the triangle and to locate the eleven symbols on it.

C. 1. Phoneticians speak of "front vowels" and "back vowels". Judging by the arrangement of the triangle, which vowels would fall in each of the two groups?

2. We sometimes call [ɔ] "open o" and [o] "close o." Can you explain why? Which is more open, [ɔ] or [ɑ]? [ɛ] or [æ]?

3. Suppose that a fellow student pronounces it as [it] instead of [ɪt]. In order to help him produce the correct sound, what would you tell him to do with his jaw, his tongue, and his lips? What would you tell him to do in order to change [gud] to [gʊd]? [gɑt] to [gɔt]?

D. Make a Viëtor triangle and number the symbols on it from 1 through 11: [i] 1, [ɪ] 2, [e] 3, etc. Your teacher will pronounce several different vowel sounds; see if you can identify each by giving the number of the symbol which represents it. If you fail to identify a vowel correctly, note on the diagram the location of the sound you thought you heard with relation to the sound the teacher actually pronounced.

E. Pronounce these very common words, and write them as they are usually spelled in English:

1. læf
2. haus
3. yɪər
4. sɔ
5. rɑk
6. sil
7. hwɑɪl
8. ðiz
9. tʃendz
10. ðɪs
11. ʃoz
12. wəns
13. lɛŋθ
14. lʊk
15. lək
16. muv
17. hwɛər
18. θɪŋ
19. dʒɔɪ
20. lɑrdʒ
21. kélər
22. ə́rlɪ
23. wɪ́mɪn
24. byútɪfʊl
25. kə́mpənɪ

Classification of Vowels

F. Can you read these phrases?
  1. hihəzfínɪʃt   3. wikənǽnsər   5. ðekə́məngó
  2. ɑɪhəvdə́nɪt   4. íꞏzɪtəsí

G. Pronounce carefully the following groups of words. They are all among the 500 most frequently used in the English language, so you are probably already familiar with their pronunciation. In each group, four words have the same vowel sound, and one has a different vowel. Draw a line under the word which does not belong with the group, and write the symbol which represents the sound the other four have in common.

  1. piece, sleep, each, bread, she.
  2. sit, been, first, him, quick.
  3. plain, death, they, great, name.
  4. learn, friend, left, head, next.
  5. add, back, have, warm, laugh.
  6. heart, watch, stop, dark, law.
  7. talk, thought, draw, cross, both.
  8. close, though, lost, road, most.
  9. book, full, put, food, should.
  10. wood, blue, two, move, do.
  11. does, foot, serve, son, bird.

H. Divide a sheet of paper into 14 columns, and write one of the following symbols at the top of each column: i, ɪ, e, ɛ, æ, ɑ, ɔ, o, ʊ, u, ə, ɑɪ, ɑʊ, ɔɪ. Classify the following words under the symbol which represents their vowel sound. If necessary, your instructor will pronounce the words for you.

  1. with   11. box   21. light   31. rain   41. out
  2. ten   12. seem   22. street   32. month   42. love
  3. strong   13. wide   23. dead   33. mean   43. put
  4. watch   14. off   24. work   34. school   44. point
  5. south   15. arm   25. look   35. best   45. were
  6. late   16. fall   26. wish   36. would   46. come
  7. bring   17. stand   27. say   37. voice   47. not
  8. good   18. bridge   28. so   38. since   48. true
  9. gold   19. through 29. those   39. glad   49. pass
  10. up   20. down   30. high   40. said   50. war

* * *

51. friend	61. heart	71. have	81. who	91. corn
52. warm	62. seize	72. touch	82. they	92. stop
53. done	63. mouth	73. could	83. miss	93. please
54. great	64. raise	74. she	84. move	94. talk
55. bone	65. cost	75. wing	85. full	95. cap
56. win	66. fence	76. front	86. wild	96. church
57. book	67. some	77. crowd	87. kept	97. most
58. law	68. foot	78. laugh	88. this	98. girl
59. act	69. lip	79. God	89. her	99. bread
60. five	70. soon	80. boy	90. car	100. give

I. Pronounce each of the columns of words you made in doing Exercise H, in order to be sure that all the words you classified together have the same vowel sound.

I. The Importance of Stress.

We put stress on a word or syllable when we pronounce the latter with such force as to give it more importance than the surrounding syllables and to make it stand out among them: for example, the *com-* of *comfortable* [kə́mfərtəbəl], or the *-ter-* of *determine* [dɪtə́rmɪn]. Stress is sometimes called accent.

A long word, such as *mathematics*, frequently has two stressed syllables, one of which is usually more prominent than the other. We then say that the most important syllable bears the primary accent, and the next most important bears the secondary accent. In the case of *mathematics*, the primary accent falls on *-mat-* and the secondary on *math-*. In a phonetic transcription, these two syllables would be marked respectively [ˊ] and [ˋ]: [mæ̀θəmǽtɪks].

Strong stresses are one of the distinguishing features of the English language; the important syllables in English are more prominent, the unimportant syllables less prominent than in most other languages. Stress then is the key to the pronunciation of an English word, and the location of the accent should always be learned with the word. If you stress the wrong syllable, it may be quite impossible for anyone listening to understand what you are trying to say.

Stress does even more than give character and rhythm to a word; it also determines to some extent the value of all its vowels -- whether an <u>a</u> is to be pronounced as [e] or [ə], for example.

II. The Pronunciation of Unstressed Vowels.

The vowel, or vowels, in a *stressed* syllable may be pronounced as [i], [ɪ], [e], [ɛ], [æ], [a], [ɔ],

[16]

[o], [ʊ], [u], [ə], [aɪ], [aʊ], [ɔɪ], etc. The vowel of an *unstressed* syllable almost always has one of two sounds: either [ə], or, less frequently, [ɪ]. No feature of English phonetics is simpler or more fundamental than this:

UNSTRESSED VOWELS ARE USUALLY PRONOUNCED [ə] OR [ɪ].

The principle may be illustrated graphically on the Viëtor triangle:

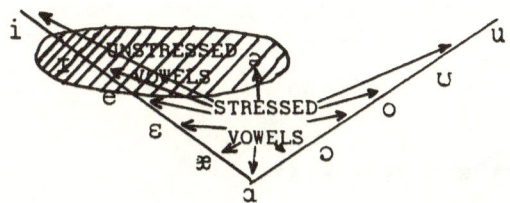

As was noted in Lesson II, [ə] is the neutral vowel, the one we produce automatically when our speech organs are relaxed, and, therefore, the one which is easiest to make. An English-speaking person is apparently willing, in a stressed syllable, to make the effort necessary to produce any of the eleven vowel sounds, but he does not feel that an unstressed syllable is important enough to justify rounding the lips, or raising or lowering the jaw. So, however he may spell the vowel sound in an unaccented syllable when he writes it, when he pronounces it he gives it the "lazy" sound of [ə], or nearby [ɪ]. Since there are more unstressed than stressed syllables in English, [ə] and [ɪ] are more frequently heard than all the other vowel sounds combined.

Notice the way in which the unaccented vowels in the following polysyllables -- words of more than one syllable -- are pronounced:

    insuperable   [ɪnsúpərəbəl]
    apparently   [əpǽrəntlɪ]
    apportionment   [əpórʃənmənt]
    congregation   [kɑ̀ŋgrɪgéʃən]
    Episcopalian   [ɪpɪ̀skəpélyən]

If a syllable bears a primary or secondary[1] accent, its vowel may be pronounced in many different ways; but only two different vowels are found in the unstressed

---

1. Unfortunately, standard English dictionaries do not always mark these secondary accents.

syllables above.

Persons who learn English as a second language almost without exception pronounce unstressed vowels too clearly. In your anxiety to make yourself understood, you will probably be tempted to say [æpǽrɛntlɪ] and [ɪpǐskopélyən]. Actually, there will be less danger of your being misunderstood, and your English will sound much more natural, if you will obscure the unstressed vowels, pronounce them [ə] or [ɪ], and make no attempt to identify them as <u>a</u>, <u>e</u>, or <u>o</u>.

Unless you consult a pronouncing dictionary or a competent English-speaking person, there is no sure way of knowing whether the unaccented vowels of an unfamiliar word should be [ə] or [ɪ]. Frequently it makes no difference; [əpǐskəpélyən] is just as natural as [ɪpǐskəpélyən].

III. Where the Stress Falls.

Unfortunately, there are no infallible rules for determining which syllable of a word should be stressed, and you will many times need to turn to the dictionary, unless you hear the word spoken by someone familiar with it. Certain observations, however, should be of help:

1. The great majority of two-syllable words are accented on the *first* syllable: *never* [névər], *breakfast* [brékfəst], *Monday* [mə́ndɪ].
2. Compound expressions:
    a. Compound *nouns* ordinarily have a primary accent on the first component and a secondary accent on the second: *bird's-nest* [bə́rdznɛ̀st], *drugstore* [drə́gstòr], *thoroughfare* [θə́rəfɛ̀ər], *weather-man* [wɛ́ðərmæ̀n].
    b. In compound *verbs* the reverse is true; there is usually a secondary accent on the first component and a primary accent on the second: *understand* [ə̀ndərstǽnd], *overlook* [òvərlúk], *outrun* [àutrə́n].
    c. In the intensive-reflexive pronouns the stronger accent also falls on the *last* syllable: *myself* [mɑ̀ɪsɛ́lf], *yourself* [yùrsɛ́lf], etc.
    d. Numbers ending in -teen may receive the stress on either syllable, but it is best for a student learning English as a second language to stress them consistently on the *last* syllable, so as to distinguish clearly between *thirty* [θə́rtɪ] and *thirteen* [θə̀rtín] *forty* [fɔ́rtɪ] and *fourteen* [fɔ̀rtín], etc.

3. A large group of words, which may be used either as nouns or verbs, have a difference in stress to indicate the difference in usage. In all such cases, the noun is accented on the first syllable, the verb on the second (compare 2-a and 2-b above).

NOUN	VERB
concert [kánsərt]	concert [kənsə́rt]
conduct [kándəkt]	conduct [kəndə́kt]
conflict [kánflɪkt]	conflict [kənflɪ́kt]
content [kántɛnt]	content [kəntɛ́nt]
contest [kántɛst]	contest [kəntɛ́st]
contract [kántrækt]	contract [kəntrǽkt]
contrast [kántræst]	contrast [kəntrǽst]
convert [kánvərt]	convert [kənvə́rt]
desert [dɛ́zərt]	desert [dɪzə́rt]
digest [dáɪdʒɛst]	digest [dɪdʒɛ́st]
exploit [ɛ́ksplɔɪt]	exploit [ɪksplɔ́ɪt]
incline [ɪ́nklaɪn]	incline [ɪnkláɪn]
increase [ɪ́nkris]	increase [ɪnkrís]
insert [ɪ́nsərt]	insert [ɪnsə́rt]
insult [ɪ́nsəlt]	insult [ɪnsə́lt]
object [ábdʒɪkt]	object [əbdʒɛ́kt]
permit [pə́rmɪt]	permit [pərmɪ́t]
present [prɛ́zənt]	present [prɪzɛ́nt]
produce [prádyus]	produce [prədyús]
progress [prágrɪs]	progress [prəgrɛ́s]
project [prádʒɪkt]	project [prədʒɛ́kt]
protest [prótɛst]	protest [prətɛ́st]
rebel [rɛ́bəl]	rebel [rɪbɛ́l]
record [rɛ́kərd]	record [rɪkɔ́rd]
survey [sə́rve]	survey [sərvé]
suspect [sə́spɛkt]	suspect [səspɛ́kt]

4. In general, when a suffix is added to a word, the new form is stressed on the same syllable as was the basic word: *abandon* [əbǽndən], *abandonment* [əbǽndənmənt]; *happy* [hǽpɪ], *happiness* [hǽpɪnɪs]; *reason* [rízən], *reasonable* [rízənəbəl]. Words ending in *-tion, -sion, -ic, -ical,* and *-ity,* however, almost always have primary stress on the syllable preceding the ending, and the addition of one of these suffixes may, therefore, result in a shift of accent: *contribute* [kəntrɪ́byət], *contribution* [kántrɪbyúʃən]; *economy* [ɪkánəmɪ], *economic* [ɪkənámɪk]; *biology* [baɪdlədʒɪ], *biological* [bàɪəládʒɪkəl]; *public* [pə́blɪk], *publicity* [pəblɪ́sɪtɪ].

IV. Exercises.

A. Your instructor will pronounce for you the following polysyllables. First decide which syllable is stressed in each case; then write down the symbols which represent all the vowel sounds in each word, and mark each stressed vowel. Example: instructor will pronounce *about* as [əbáʊt]; student writes 1. ə-áʊ.

1. about
2. across
3. after
4. again
5. another
6. begin
7. between
8. children
9. family
10. general
11. hundred
12. letter
13. many
14. measure
15. mother
16. often
17. receive
18. remember
19. something
20. sometime
21. story
22. thousand
23. together
24. visit
25. without

B. Arrange in separate lists the vowels that you heard in stressed syllables and those that you found in unstressed syllables. Are your results in agreement with Section II of this Lesson? Can you explain the apparent violation of the rule found in *sometime* [sə́mtaɪm]?

C. In order to increase your ability to recognize and place stresses, read this drill after your instructor, and then alone. Watch carefully the pronunciation of unstressed vowels. Note that words with a similar pattern of stresses are grouped together; each group should be repeated rhythmically:

a. 1́-2
1. bury
2. judgment
3. dollar
4. minus
5. nation

b. 1-2́
1. around
2. occur
3. submit
4. disease
5. deceive

c. 1́-2-3
1. vigilance
2. readiness
3. mineral
4. emphasis
5. similar

d. 1-2́-3
1. distinguish
2. abandon
3. eraser
4. delicious
5. paternal

e. 1́-2-3́
1. overlook
2. evermore
3. premature
4. magazine
5. guarantee

f. 1́-2-3-4
1. memorable
2. personally
3. accuracy
4. amicably
5. delicacy

g. 1-2́-3-4
1. mechanical
2. immediate
3. absurdity
4. catastrophe
5. additional

h. 1́-2-3́-4
1. corporation
2. education
3. sentimental
4. scientific
5. economic

i. 1́-2-3́-4-5
1. mathematical
2. zoölogical
3. nationality
4. anniversary
5. indeterminate

j. 1-2́-3-4́-5
1. communication
2. eradication
3. pronunciation
4. deliberation
5. appropriation

D. Pronounce these very common words, and write

them as they are usually spelled in English:

1. ʃɪp
2. θæŋk
3. on
4. drap
5. sun
6. ɪst
7. ples
8. sɛz
9. brɔt
10. tʃɔrtʃ
11. hwaɪ
12. gʊd
13. vɔɪs
14. naʊ
15. fiəld
16. lərnd
17. krɔst
18. wɔntɪd
19. sépərɪt
20. læŋgwɪdʒ
21. néʃən
22. pɪ́ktʃər
23. ənéf
24. sévrəl
25. évrɪ

E. Can you read these phrases?
   1. təðəléft
   2. ɔnətrɪ́p
   3. gɪvɪttəmɪ́
   4. ɪfwihədnɔ́n
   5. mǽnənwɑ́rʃ

F. Pronounce these families of words, paying particular attention to the location of the stresses and to t vowels in unstressed syllables (See Section III-4 of this Lesson):
   1. abominate [əbɑ́mɪnét], abominable, abominableness, abomination.
   2. contribute [kəntrɪ́byət], contributor, contribution, contributive.
   3. abolish [əbɑ́lɪʃ], abolition, abolishable, abolitionist.
   4. electric [əléktrɪk], electrical, electricity, electrify.
   5. apology [əpɑ́lədʒɪ], apologetic, apologize.
   6. attain [ətén], attainable, attainability, attainment.
   7. material [mətɪ́rɪəl], materialist, materialistic, materialize.
   8. philosophy [fɪlɑ́səfɪ], philosopher, philosophical, philosophize.
   9. method [méθəd], methodical, Methodist.
   10. negotiate [nɪgóʃɪét], negotiable, negotiation, negotiator, negotiability.

G. Mark the accent on all words of more than one syllable (see Section III - 2 and 3 of this Lesson), then pronounce the following sentences several times:
   1. Would you object if I gave her the present myself?
   2. I don't understand why the class should protest or rebel.
   3. No one suspected that the runner had made a new record.
   4. They will need a permit to exploit the mine themselves.

5. What an exploit! Sixty miles in sixteen minutes!
6. The conflict is over, and the coal miners have a new contract.
7. What progress are they making with their survey?
8. It's hard to content rebels.
9. The "Digest" is conducting a contest to increase its circulation.
10. How was his conduct at the concert?
11. I'm trying to digest the contents of fifteen books.
12. So far they have been unable to produce any suspects.
13. You will convert no one by insults.
14. Will you yourself conduct the project?

H. Read aloud several pages of English, concentrating your attention on the pronunciation of the unstressed vowels in words of more than one syllable.

LESSON IV

Sentence-Stress and Rhythm

I. **Stress in Groups of Words.**

In Lesson III, we were concerned with the stressing of syllables in words of more than one syllable. word-stress. Our knowledge of stress must, however, go beyond words, if we are to have the complete picture. We do not really talk in words, most of the time, but in sentences, or at least phrases.

In the sentence *I am glad to see you*, there are normally two stresses: on *glad* and *see*. Since these are words of only one syllable, they have no word-stress, but the emphasis that is put on them is in many ways the same as that put on the first syllable of *history* [hístərɪ]. It is sometimes convenient, however, to distinguish between word-stress (history) and sentence-stress (I am glad to see you).

When sentence-stress falls on a word of more than one syllable, it always falls on the syllable which normally receives word-stress: "I'll meet you tomorrow."

In Lesson III it was pointed out that there is a great deal more difference in English than in most other languages between stressed and unstressed syllables; this is as true of sentence-stress as of word stress. To an English-speaking person the rhythm of many other tongues (particularly French, Spanish, Italian, Tagalog) sounds mechanically regular — a series of little bursts of sound all of about the same size and force, like machine-gun fire. English pronounced with such a rhythm would probably not be understood. If asked to draw a picture representing the rhythm of the syllables in Spanish, the speaker of English might produce a line of soldiers of very much the same size and following one another at rather regular intervals.

The Rhythm of Some Other Languages

His own language he might picture as a series of family groups, each composed of a parent accompanied by several small children of varying sizes. A few of the adults might be childless, and some would be larger than others.

The Rhythm of English

In a language like French or Spanish, a line of poetry is usually determined by counting the total number of syllables, stressed and unstressed alike. Lines containing the same number of syllables are felt to be of the same length. In a line of English poetry the number of sentence-stresses is more important than the number of syllables. Here are two verses from Tennyson, which are considered to be perfectly matched and of the same length:

"Bréak, bréak, bréak,
 On thy cóld gray stónes, O Séa!"

The unstressed syllables are so unimportant, rhythmi-

cally speaking, that it is not even necessary to count
them. When a person recites those lines, it takes him
as long to say the first as the second, even though the
first contains only three syllables and the second is
made up of seven.

This leads to a significant observation regarding
English pronunciation: ACCENTS TEND TO RECUR AT REGU-
LAR INTERVALS. The more unstressed syllables there are
between accents, the more rapidly (and indistinctly)
they are pronounced. This is true to a large extent
even of prose.

Have your teacher or a native speaker of English
pronounce these two sentences for you at normal speed:

>   The bóy is ínterested in enlárging his
>   vocábulary.
>
>   Gréat prógress is máde dáily.

Note how he instinctively crushes together the unstressed
syllables of the first sentence in order to get
them said in time, and how he lengthens somewhat the
stressed syllables of the second so as to compensate
for the lack of intervening unstressed syllables.

The problem of acquiring a good English speech
rhythm may be divided into five parts:

1. Giving proper emphasis to stressed syllables,
   and making them recur rather regularly within a thought group.
2. Weakening unstressed words and syllables, and
   obscuring the vowels in many of them.
3. Proper organization of words into thought
   groups by means of pauses.
4. Blending the final sound of each word and
   syllable with the initial sound of the one
   following within a thought group.
5. Fitting the entire sentence into a normal intonation pattern.

Intonation patterns will be studied in Lessons V and VI,
and the rest of this lesson will treat the other four
phases of the problem.

II. Which Words Should be Stressed?

Grammarians sometimes divide all words into two
classes: 1) *content words*, which have meaning in themselves, like *mother, forget,* and *tomorrow;* and 2) *function words*, which have little or no meaning other than
the grammatical idea they express, such as *the, of,* and
will. In general content words are stressed, but *func-*

tion words are left *unstressed*, unless the speaker wishes to call special attention to them.

Content words, usually *stressed*, include:
1. Nouns.
2. Verbs (except those listed under function words).
3. Adjectives.
4. Adverbs.
5. Demonstratives: *this, that, these, those.*
6. Interrogatives: *who, when, why,* etc.

Function words, usually *unstressed*, include:
1. Articles: *a, an, the.*
2. Prepositions: *to, of, in,* etc.
3. Personal pronouns: *I, me, he, him, it,* etc.
4. Possessive adjectives: *my, his, your,* etc.
5. Relative pronouns: *who, that, which,* etc.
6. Common conjunctions: *and, but, that, as, if,* etc.
7. *One* used as a noun-substitute: as in *the red dress* and *the blue one.*
8. The verbs *be, have, do, will, would, shall, should, can, could, may, might,* and *must.* (These are easy to remember, since they are the verbs which may be used as auxiliaries and substitutes for other verbs.)

Though all nouns are actually *content* words, the first of two nouns used together ordinarily receives sentence-stress while the second does not: *an apartment house, business affairs* (compare Lesson III, Section III, 2-a).

Though most verbs are also *content* words, in two-word verbs made up of a verb and adverb it is normally the *adverb* which receives sentence-stress, not the *verb*: *to split up, to put on* (compare Lesson III, Section III, 2-b). Do not confuse these genuine two-word verbs with other verbs, like *look* and *listen*, which may be followed by a prepositional phrase: *to look at him, to listen to him.* A good way to tell the difference between, for example, *to put on* and *to look at* is to put both expressions in a question beginning with *what*: *What are you putting on? What are you looking at?* Note that *at* may be placed before *what* and thus separated from the verb: *At what are you looking?* But the two-word verb cannot be divided in this way: *On what are you putting?* does not make sense.

By means of its stressed syllables, a thought group (or a sentence made up of several thought groups) may be analyzed as a series of rhythm units. A rhythm unit must contain one stressed syllable -- that is, one con-

tent word -- and it may include one or several unstressed syllables also. The stressed syllable comes at the end of the unit, except that one or more unstressed syllables may be attached after the *final* stress in the thought group. Function words are counted merely as unstressed syllables. Note carefully how the rhythm units of the following sentences are made up:
1. She declares /[1]that she likes / rats.
2. I don't imáǵine he can succeed / in a business.
3. In an hour / I shall deliver it to you.

Which are the content words? Which are the function words? Can you find the word which is a part of two rhythm units? The rhythm unit made up of only one syllable? Examples of unstressed syllables at the end of a rhythm unit?

Naturally, some of these same sentences might be combined into different rhythm units by various speakers and under various circumstances. It seems that many speakers prefer rhythm units which contain two or three unstressed syllables. Such persons may feel that *rats* in Sentence 1 above is not long enough to be treated as a separate unit; if *likes* appears to them more important than *rats*, the stress on the latter may be suppressed and *rats* may become simply an unstressed syllable attached to the end of the preceding unit: *She declares / that she likes rats*. Similarly, a speaker may feel that *I shall deliver it to you* in Sentence 3 is too long to be a rhythm unit, and break it into two units by stressing *to*, even though *to* is only a function word: *I shall delivér it to you*.

The usual rhythm units are frequently changed too if the speaker wishes to call special attention to one of the normally unstressed words of the thought group. If the speaker of Sentence 2 wishes to suggest that *he* cannot succeed though perhaps someone else could, *he* may be stressed and the thought group divided into four units rather than the normal three: *I don't imáǵine he / can succeed / in a business*.

The possibility of these unusual divisions need not, however, disturb the person who is learning English as a second language. In the great majority of cases, sentence-stresses are placed normally, as indicated at the beginning of this section.

III. Pronunciation of Unstressed Words of One Syllable.

The group of unstressed words of one syllable includes most of the commonest words in the language; the

1. This diagonal line does *not* represent a pause.

ten most frequently used words all belong in that class: *the*, *of*, *and*, *to*, *a*, *in*, *that*, *it*, *is*, and *I*. These ten make up twenty-five percent of all that is written and spoken in English. Or, putting it another way, one out of every four words we use will be *the*, or *of*, or *and*, etc. Unfortunately, several of the ten are among the most generally mispronounced of all English words. It is probable that in no other way can you improve your English so much and so easily as by learning to pronounce them perfectly.

The rhythm pattern made up of the alternation of stressed and unstressed syllables is powerfully reinforced in English by the phenomenon known as the obscuring of vowels. By pronouncing the vowel of an unstressed syllable obscurely, as [ə] or [ɪ], a speaker weakens that syllable still further and increases the contrast between it and stressed syllables. We have already seen, in Lesson III, how obscuring works in polysyllables. As might be expected, it occurs also in quite a few words of only one syllable when these latter do not receive sentence-stress.

THERE IS A STRONG TENDENCY TO OBSCURE THE VOWELS OF THE MOST COMMON UNSTRESSED WORDS OF ONE SYLLABLE JUST AS THE UNACCENTED VOWELS OF POLYSYLLABLES ARE OBSCURED; THAT IS, TO PRONOUNCE THEM [ə] OR [ɪ].

Thus, contrary to what is taught in most beginning English classes the world over, the indefinite article *a* is ordinarily [ə], not [e]: *in a minute* [ɪn ə mɪnɪt]. Only in a few rare cases is *a* stressed, and given the clear sound [e]: *the article "a"* [ðɪ ártɪkəl é].

There are, then, two separate pronunciations of this and other similar words: one obscured, and one clear. A list of such words is given below:

Word	Obscured Sound	Example	Clear Sound
* a	[ə]	in *a* car [ɪn ə kar]	[e]
* an	[ən]	get *an* egg [gɛt ən ɛg]	[æn]
* and	[ən]	high *and* low [haɪ ən lo]	[ænd]
are	[ər]	two *are* ready [tu ər rédɪ]	[ar]
can	[kən]	you *can* come [yu kən kəm]	[kæn]
had	[həd]	I *had* been [aɪ həd bɪn]	[hæd]
has	[həz]	it *has* gone [ɪt həz gɔn]	[hæz]
have	[həv]	we *have* seen [wi həv sin]	[hæv]
* of	[əv]	three *of* us [θri əv əs]	[av]
* or	[ər]	one *or* two [wən ər tu]	[ɔr]
that	[ðət]	those *that* went [ðoz ðət wɛnt]	[ðæt]
* the	[ðə] or [ðɪ]	on *the* right [ɔn ðə raɪt]	[ði]
* to	[tə]	five *to* two [faɪv tə tu]	[tu]
was	[wəz]	it *was* late [ɪt wəz let]	[waz]

Pronounce the examples many times, until they sound perfectly natural to you.

The words on the list which are marked with an asterisk (*) are almost always obscured: *a, an, and, of, or, the,* and *to.*

That is obscured when used as a relative pronoun or a conjunction: *the word that you want* [ðə wə́rd ðət yu wɔ́nt], *I know that he will* [aɪ nó ðə̆t hi wɪ́əl]. It is stressed and pronounced [ðǽt] as a demonstrative: *the reason for that* [ðə rízən fɔr ðǽt].

The verbs *are, can, had, has, have,* and *was* are usually obscured, but are given their clear pronunciation at the end of a clause or sentence: *Who was here? John was.* [hú wə́z hɪ́ər? dʒán wɑ́z]. *Can* has the added peculiarity of being pronounced with [æ], rather than [ə], in the contraction *can't*: *I can't tell you* [aɪ kǽnt tśəl yu]. Since the final [t], as normally pronounced in a combination like *can't tell,* is nearly impossible to hear, a person listening to the sentence would understand it as negative or positive depending on whether he heard [æ] *(can't)* or [ə] *(can)*. The obscuring of vowels can indeed affect meaning!

The vowels of many other unstressed words of one syllable *may* be obscured; the words listed above are those it is most necessary to obscure in order to avoid a "foreign accent."

IV. Thought Groups.

The expression "thought groups" refers, not to the rhythm units we have until now been mostly concerned with in this lesson, but to larger groupings of words which are determined by the meaning of the sentence. Thought groups are set apart by pauses, and are often composed of several rhythm units. These pauses may be indicated by a double diagonal line, //, easily distinguishable from the single line, /, used to show rhythm units: *If you will come / at once,// there may be time / for a swim.//*

It is impossible to make a complete set of "rules" for the division of a sentence into thought groups; there is no one "right" or even "normal" way of distributing the pauses. It is probable that in no other element of their speech do individual speakers vary so widely. Logically, a "thought group" should contain what the speaker feels to be a single thought. If the sentence is being read, the author's punctuation will show at least some of the pauses he wished to have made. But punctuation is not an infallible guide, and of course most speech is not read. If pauses are made too frequently, the effect is unpleasant; if they are made too infrequently, the speaker runs out of breath.

This great freedom in making pauses does not mean, however, that they may occur between any two words in a sentence. A pause normally comes at the end of a rhythm unit. Pauses may be made within the rhythm unit only after the first syllable or two, when these are very closely connected with the preceding sentence-stress. Thus in the sentence, "Phras/ing depends / upon the mean/ing of what you say", there should be no pause after *upon, the, of, what,* and *you;* but there may be one after *phrasing, depends,* or *meaning* Other examples of syllables closely enough connected with the preceding sentence-stress to permit pausing within a rhythm unit are:

1. The last of two nouns used together: *There's a ball / game at eight / o'clock / tonight* (pause possible after *game*).
2. Pronoun objects of a preceding verb: *He prom/ised to see / me as soon / as possible* (pause possible after *me*).

Even at the end of a rhythm unit a pause should not be made if it would separate words very closely united grammatically or logically, such as:

1. A noun and the word which modifies it: *It's cer/tainly a beau/tiful day* (no pause after *beautiful*).
2. A noun and the prepositional phrase which modifies it: *I wish / I had a deck / of cards* (no pause after *deck*).

The two preceding paragraphs are, of course, simply another and more concrete way of saying that pauses may occur between the large grammatical divisions of a sentence, but not between parts that are very closely dependent on each other. Within these limits the student of English may enjoy his freedom to make thought groups as he pleases. It is most important, nevertheless, that he should make definite groups. A student's most frequent error with regard to grouping is probably failure to organize what he says into clear-cut groups of any sort. Without pauses or organization a long English sentence, with its nearly regular recurrence of word-stresses, becomes intolerably monotonous and may even be unintelligible.

Within thought groups, words and syllables are not pronounced as separate units; they flow along smoothly,

without jerkiness, and one seems to blend into the next.
A person who did not know any English would find it
hard to tell where one word ended and another began.
The blending between the two words of *read it* is as
close as that between the two syllables of *reading*.
Within a thought group a speaker does not completely
interrupt, even for a second, the outward flow of his
breath. The blending is accomplished by this uninter-
rupted flow of breath, and by the fact that even while
one sound is being formed the speech organs are already
moving on to the position in which the next is to be
formed.

   Those who are learning English as a second language often spoil the blending within thought groups by
inserting little puffs of air or [ə]-sounds in order to
divide combinations of consonants which seem difficult
to them: *I don't think so* [ɑɪ dontə θɪŋkə so]. (This
phenomenon is treated in some detail in Lesson VIII,
Sections III and IV). Blending may also be spoiled by
making glottal stops, that is by cutting off completely
the outflow of breath for an instant by closing the
glottis (the vocal cords). Glottal stops, indicated by
the symbol [ʔ] are rare in normal English, occurring
regularly in only a few special combinations like *oh,oh*
[oʔo] (to express dismay). In some other languages (German) they are quite common, and may even serve to distinguish between one word and another (Danish, Tagalog).
The student of English should not use glottal stops to
separate vowel from vowel or consonant from vowel: for
example, the [i] and [o] of *be over* [bi ovər] should be
blended.

V. Exercises.

   A. Do you understand the meaning of the following
      phrases? Each is a rhythm unit of the sort that
      makes up most of our speech. Each is written as
      one word, and in actual conversation, with blend-
      ing well done, would be pronounced as one word.
      Pronounce the phrases several times, making the
      contrast between stressed and unstressed sylla-
      bles very strong. The ten most common English
      words are all used here, those which make up
      twenty-five percent of all that is said and writ-
      ten in English. As a foundation for future prog-
      ress, can you learn to pronounce at least these
      ten words perfectly?
      1. əvðəlésən   5. ɪzəfrénd
      2. əvðədé   6. ɪzəkwéstʃən
      3. əvəwə́rd   7. ɪzənǽnsər
      4. ɪnəbə́s   8. ɪzðətrúθ

9. ðətwinó
10. ðózðətkém
11. təbihǽpɪ
12. təhəvmɛ́tyu
13. yuhəvtóldmi
14. hihəzbɪnsín
15. ɑrhədθót
16. ɑrkəndúrt
17. ɪtwəzdén
18. wiərgóɪŋ
19. fɑ́ɪvərsíks
20. yúənmí

B. Pronounce each of the following expressions as a
blended unit, just as you did the transcribed
phrases of the preceding exercise. Be very careful to weaken and obscure unstressed syllables
properly. Sentence-stress is marked in each
case.

-1-
a. supplánt
b. the plánt
c. the tónes
d. that ówns
e. the begínning
f. that you go
g. in the máil
h. on the róad
i. with the óthers
j. for the perfórmance

-2-
a. unáble
b. a náme
c. an áim
d. an órange
e. a stúdy
f. in a húrry
g. in a móment
h. for a náp
i. for an ápple
j. at a garáge

-3-
a. of the wár
b. of the péace
c. of his stóry
d. of a réstaurant
e. of a proféssor
f. is of úse
g. will be of sérvice
h. is míschievous
i. the rést of us
j. the sóund of it

-4-
a. todáy
b. to tówn
c. to trý
d. to énter
e. to belóng
f. to be fóund
g. to the bóard
h. to an énd
i. I cáme to him
j. he sáid to me

-5-
a. perfórmed
b. are fórmed
c. are bróken
d. are allówed
e. are a fámily
f. we are thánkful
g. I was ríght
h. she was afráid
i. was the spéaker
j. was a béauty

-6-
a. submít
b. had míssed
c. had léft
d. has bráught
e. has devéloped
f. it has ópened
g. have becóme
h. have been decíd-
   ed
i. would have líked
j. may have cáught it

-7-
a. consént

-8-
a. arrést

  b. can sénd   b. or rést
  c. can téll you   c. or a Cámel
  d. can defénd   d. understánd
  e. can have háppened e. óne or twó
  f. he can dánce   f. uncértain
  g. I can sée it   g. and cértainly
  h. I can't sée it   h. and he díd it
  i. you can trúst him i. bláck and blúe
  j. you can't trúst him j. Jámes and Í

C. Here are four series of sentences, with sentence-stresses and rhythm units marked. In each series except the last, sentence *b* contains more syllables than sentence *a*, sentence *c* more than sentence *b*, etc., but the number of rhythm units is always the same: the addition of the extra syllables does not mean any appreciable lengthening in the time it takes to say the entire sentence (see Section I of this lesson). Tap on a table with your pencil, slowly and regularly, in groups of three beats. Then pronounce each series of sentences several times, making a stressed syllable fall on each beat, and bringing in all unstressed syllables between beats. Each time you read, tap a little faster.

      -1-
 a. Dógs / éat / bónes.
 b. The dógs / éat / bónes.
 c. The dógs / will éat / bónes.
 d. The dógs / will éat / the bónes.
 e. The dógs / will have éat/en the bónes.

      -2-
 a. The cár / is hére / nów.
 b. The cár / is out frónt / nów.
 c. The cár / will be out frónt / in a móment.
 d. The cár / will be in the garáge / in a moment.

      -3-
 a. Bóys / néed / móney.
 b. The bóys / will néed / móney.
 c. The bóys / will néed / some móney.
 d. The bóys / will be néed/ing some móney.
 e. The bóys / will be néed/ing some of their móney.

      -4-
 a. A drúg/store's the pláce / to have lúnch.
 b. We shall sóon / finish úp / for the seméster.

c. June / is a nice / month.
d. It's the most excíting perfórmance you've ever seen!
e. Great / day / in the morning!

D. The passage below, in ordinary conversational style, is to be prepared for rhythmic reading by:
1. Marking all normal sentence-stresses (see Section II of this lesson).
   a. *Forget-Me-Not* (in Sentence 2) is a compound noun, and the indefinite pronoun *anything* (3 and 5) is like a compound noun; where should they be stressed (Lesson III, Section III, 2-a)?
   b. Where should the intensive pronoun *themselves* (7) be stressed (Lesson III, Section III, 2-c)?
   c. *Card game* (6) is an example of two nouns used together; position of stress (Section II of this lesson)?
   d. *Call out* (3 and 6), and *put down* (3 and 6) are two-word verbs; position of stress (Section II of this lesson)? Are *comes to* (3) and *think of* (5) two-word verbs?
   e. Would you stress *because* (7), *you* (8), *is* (8)? Why, or why not?
2. Combining the words into rhythm units by means of the symbol (/).
   a. Do you find any cases of several very short rhythm units coming together? What could you do about *say / each / word* (3) (Section II of this lesson)?
   b. Do you feel that *Or if I call out / "bridge"* (6) is a difficult or unnatural rhythmic combination? If so, how else could the phrase be stressed?
   c. If you were the speaker, do you think you would want to call special attention to *I* and *you* in Sentences 5 and 6?
3. Combining rhythm units into thought groups, and indicating the latter by inserting (//) where pauses should be made (Section IV of this lesson).
   a. Would you pause after *that* (1), *first* (3), *green* (5)? Why, or why not?
   b. Sentence 1 is almost too long to read without a pause; would it be better to break it after *game* or *play*? Why?

American English Pronunciation 35

Would you break Sentence 7 after *people* or *things*?

Passage for Reading

1. There's a little game I want us to play that I used to play at school. 2. It's called Forget-Me-Not. 3. I'm going to call out some words -- just anything at all -- and as I say each word, you're all to put down the first thing that comes to your mind. 4. Is that clear? 5. For instance, if I should say "grass," you might write "it's green," or anything else you think of. 6. Or if I call out "bridge," you might put down "a card game." 7. It's an interesting game because it shows the reactions of people to different things and tells you a lot about the people themselves. 8. You see how simple and easy it is?

Adapted from *You Can't Take It With You* by Moss Hart and George S. Kaufman, copyright, 1937, by Moss Hart and George S. Kaufman, and reprinted by permission of the publishers, Rhinehart & Company, Inc.

Naturally it is not expected or desired that all students should mark this passage alike. After you have marked it, read it several times, making sentence stresses recur rhythmically and blending the words in each thought group. If the teacher finds that you tend to break up thought groups with glottal stops or otherwise, it may help you prevent this if you will draw a line linking words or syllables between which you are likely to interrupt the flow of breath: say each (3), different things (7).

E. Mark the stresses in the sentences which appear below, and transcribe each sentence in phonetic symbols. Write each word separately, rather than running words together in phrases as in Exercise A. After you have made your transcription, your instructor will pronounce the exercise, so that you may check your transcription with his pronunciation. Pay particular attention to the obscured and clear sounds of verbs which may be used as auxiliaries, such as *can* and *have*. Finally, practice reading the material from your corrected transcription.

1. What can I give as an answer?
2. I'm afraid it will be hard to do.
3. He says that he will come if he can.
4. I thought she would be pretty, and she was.
5. She has worked with children since the end of the war.

6. Men have shown no patience with it, but women have.
7. The car had been brought, and was ready to use.
8. If I had seen you sooner, we could have gone together.

F. There follow three stanzas of a well-known poem. Its natural rhythm is so compelling that it may help you learn to make stressed syllables recur regularly and to obscure unstressed syllables. Mark the sentence-stresses, with your instructor's help if necessary; note what types of words are stressed and unstressed, and check your findings with Section II of this lesson. Why do you suppose *give* is left unstressed? Read the poem many times, being particularly careful of the way in which you pronounce such words as *a* and *can*; or, better still, memorize the selection.

Give a Man a Horse He Can Ride
James Thomson (1834-1882)

Give a man a horse he can ride,
Give a man a boat he can sail;
And his rank and wealth, his strength and health
On sea nor shore shall fail.

Give a man a pipe he can smoke,
Give a man a book he can read;
And his home is bright with a calm delight,
Though the rooms be poor indeed.

Give a man a girl he can love,
As I, O my Love, love thee;
And his hand is great with the pulse of Fate,
At home, on land, on Sea.

G. If facilities are available, the class could make a recording of "Give a Man a Horse He Can Ride". Naturally, the selection should first be rehearsed many times, as a choral reading; this careful preparation, motivated by the recording, is the chief value of the exercise. The first two lines of Stanza I, which deal with outdoor life, might be assigned to an individual, a man with an energetic, bass voice; the last two lines to the entire class. In Stanza II, which speaks of indoor activities, the first two lines could be read by another man, with a somewhat lighter and more contemplative way of speaking. If a longer passage is desired for the recording, the three stanzas above might be preceded by another poem of Thomson's, the one which begins, "I looked out into the morning."

H. While working on this lesson, each student should read aloud, with attention concentrated on sentence-stress and rhythm, as many passages as possible from other books he is studying.

LESSON V

Rising-Falling Intonation

I. What Intonation Is.

Intonation is the tune of what we say. More specifically, it is the combination of musical tones on which we pronounce the syllables that make up our speech. It is closely related to sentence-stress. Often, but by no means always, a syllable with sentence-stress is spoken on a higher musical note than the rest of the rhythm unit. In such cases, intonation is one of the elements of stress, the others being loudness and length.

It is possible to identify on a piano or other musical instrument the note or notes on which any given syllable is pronounced. Good speakers sometimes use as many as twenty-five different notes to give variety and meaning to what they say. Others may use a much smaller range. We could, then, mark the intonation of sentences by writing them below the proper notes on a staff, as a song is written.

Have you ever listened to the tune of your own voice? What tune do you use when you say "What time is it?" and "Good morning"? Can you identify any of the notes on a piano? Which word did you pronounce on the highest note? Which word or syllable on the lowest note? Can you draw a line which will show the tune of *What time is it?* by rising and falling at the proper places?

Each speaker has his own range of notes, and it is not necessary in order to pronounce English well for you to imitate someone else's intonation, note for note. What is important is not that a given syllable be pronounced on the note *do* and another on *re*, but the direction of the shift between syllables, the general movement of the voice up or down. Most native speakers of English, under similar circumstances and pronouncing the same words, would make their voices rise or fall at approximately the same places.

It will be sufficient for our purposes if we divide the tones used for intonation into three types: normal, high, and low. We can then mark the movements of the voice up or down by drawing lines at three different levels over or under the passage we are explaining. A line drawn *at the base of the letters* of a word indicates that that word is pronounced on a *normal* tone, a line *above the word* marks a *high* tone, and a line *some distance below the word* marks a *low* tone. Can you make your voice follow the lines?

How are you, Mr. Johnson?

I'll have cream and sugar.

Usually the movement from one tone to another takes place *between syllables*, and is called a *shift*. Shifts are indicated by a *straight vertical line*, as that between *how* and *are* in the first example above, or that between *are* and *you*. Sometimes, however, the voice slides from one tone to another while it is pronouncing a syllable; such movement *within a syllable* is marked by a *line curving up or down*, and is known as an *inflection*.

all day long

In this last example, we begin to pronounce *long* on a note higher than normal, and then the voice slides down to a note lower than normal before the end of the syllable.

II. Rising-Falling Intonation.

Correct intonation seems to be most necessary at the end of a sentence. In this position, the voice most frequently rises above normal, then falls below normal. This means that the rising-falling intonation pattern looks like this:

or this:

The key to such a pattern is the location of the high note: what comes immediately *before* this high note is spoken on a *normal* pitch, and what comes *after* is spoken on a *low* pitch. In a short sentence, if you know where to put the high note, the rest of the pattern falls automatically into place.

THE HIGH NOTE NORMALLY COINCIDES WITH THE LAST SENTENCE-STRESS.

Note these examples:

The situátion is intólerable.

I sáid I couldn't héar you.

In both of the sentences above there are, after the last sentence-stress and its high note, one or more unstressed syllables left to receive the low note. The downward movement of the voice is then a shift, shown by a vertical line between the syllable with the high note and the following syllable. In some cases, on the other hand, the last sentence-stress and its high note may come on the very last syllable, leaving no room for the low note which must follow: as in *The dinner is cold*. It is then that the voice makes an inflection, shown by a curved line. Both the high and the low notes are heard as the last syllable is pronounced, and the voice slides down from the high to the low note within the syllable, the phenomenon referred to at the end of Section I of this lesson.

The dínner is cóld.

Whát tíme did you cáll?

This sliding from one note to another *within* a single stressed syllable means that the vowel of the syllable will be held for a comparatively long time, so long that it may break into two slightly different vowels -- a diphthong. If we were trying to represent the sounds as closely as possible, the above examples might be transcribed as:

ðə dɪnər ɪz kould.   (rather than [kold])

hwát táɪm dɪd yu koul?   (rather than [kol])

These two-toned syllables and the consequent diphthongization constitute one of the important differences between English and many other languages. Here intonation and pronunciation meet. The proper use of inflections will make it much easier to give normal diphthongal quality to the right vowels.

The fact that the high note normally coincides with the last sentence-stress may enable us, in speaking, to distinguish between such expressions as *blackbird* (a certain species of bird) and *black bird* (any bird black in color):

I saw a blackbird.

I saw a black bird.

Why does the high note come on different syllables in these two examples? Why is the downward movement of the voice a shift in the first case, and an inflection in the second?

IN ENGLISH, RISING-FALLING INTONATION IS NORMALLY USED AT THE END OF:

1. SIMPLE STATEMENTS OF FACT (DECLARATIVE SENTENCES)

   This is my wife.

   He hasn't said a word.

2. COMMANDS

   Come to see me.

3. QUESTIONS WHICH BEGIN WITH AN INTERROGATIVE WORD, SUCH AS *WHAT, WHO, WHY*, ETC.[1]

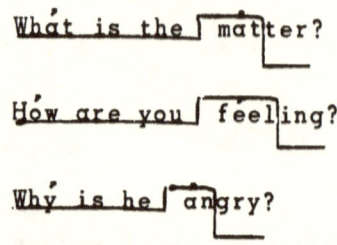

Persons whose native language is not English may have considerable difficulty at first in pronouncing questions of the type just described with the proper rising-falling intonation. The tendency to use a rising intonation in such cases must be strongly resisted.

The fall of your voice to a low tone at the end of a sentence is a sort of vocal punctuation mark, a vocal period, indicating that the thought is completed. A listener feels that there is more to be added until he hears your voice drop. A disagreeable and puzzling impression of inconclusiveness is given the listener when a speaker's voice falls only a little or not at all at the end of a statement, command, or question beginning with an interrogative word. Clear rising-falling intonation establishes a mood of certainty and completeness.

III. Exercises.

A. Listen carefully as your instructor pronounces some of the material below. Can you hear the high and low notes in his voice? Then, in order to fix the rising-falling intonation pattern in your mind, ear, and speech habits, repeat these short sentences yourself until they sound perfectly natural to you. Make your voice follow the intonation line, and do not forget to obscure unstressed vowels and to blend words together.

1. I'd like an apple.   2. I'd like a sandwich.

---

[1] Grammarians call these "special questions," and distinguish them from "general questions," which do not begin with an interrogative word. General questions, such as *Are you coming?*, may be answered by *yes* or *no*; special questions, such as *What time is it?*, require more specific information as an answer.

3. I'd like a soda.

4. I'd like some coffee.

5. I'd like a hot dog.

6. I'd like a wrist watch.

7. I'd like to hear it.

8. I'd like to be there.

9. I'd like to forget them.

10. I'd like to believe it.

11. I'd like to come over.

12. I'd like a newspaper.

13. I'd like to answer him.

14. I'd like to speak to you.

15. I'd like a balcony seat.

16. I'd like a ring.

17. I'd like an "A".

18. I'd like to see.

19. I'd like to leave.

20. I'd like to know.

21. I'd like a cigarette.

22. I'd like to find out.

23. I'd like to finish up.

24. I'd like a new car.

25. I'd like a bowl of soup.

B. This exercise is to be done as you did the preceding one. It may take you longer, however, to make these "special" questions sound completely natural with rising-falling intonation.

1. What did you do?

2. What did you find?

3. What did you want?

4. What did you ask?

5. What did you forget?

6. What did you think up?

7. What did you think of?

8. What did you run over?

9. What did you tell her?

10. What did you speak about?

11. What is he carrying?

12. What is he giving you?

13. What is he waiting for?

14. What is he studying it for?

15. What is he talking about?

16. How do you do?

17. How are you feeling?

18. Who wrote it?

19. Which is the library?

20. Why did you do it?

21. When do we eat?

22. Which ones are the best?

23. When can I study?

24. Whom did you want to speak with?

25. Where's the Physics Building?

C. First, read over the following exercise silently to make sure you understand the meaning of each sentence. Then pronounce the entire series several times, concentrating on rhythm and intonation.

1. ɑɪm ˈhæŋgrɪ.

2. ɑɪ tʊk ɪt.

3. hɑu mətʃ ɪz ɪt?

4. ɪts ðɛər vəkeʃən.

5. hwʌt du yu wɑnt?

6. hɑu du yu du.

7. ðæt wɪəl bi faɪn.

8. rɪŋ fɔr ðə bɔɪ.

9. gɪv hɪm ə tɪp.

10. ðɪs ɪz nyu yɔrk.

11. hwʌt kən ɪt bɪ?

12. pɛ fɔr ɪt nɑu.

13. kʌm tə ðə wɪndo.

14. hwɛr ər yu lɛfɪŋ?

15. hwɛər ɪz ðə dɪnɪŋ rum?

16. hu ɪz æt ðə dɔr?

17. tɛ́əl hɪm tə kəm ɪ́n.

18. ɑɪ níd ə rʌ́m.

19. ɪts nɪ́ar ðə hótəl.

20. ɑɪm rɛ́dɪ tə gɵ́.

21. ʃi hæŋ ʌ́p ðə drɛ́s.

22. ðɛərz ə tɛ́ləfon ɪn ðə kɔ́rnər.

23. rɑ́ɪt yur ném hɪ́ər.

24. wi tɛ́k aur miəlz hɪ́ər.

25. hú brɔ́t ðə bǽgz?

D. Be very careful in placing the high note as you pronounce the following pairs of sentences:
1. a. In Pasadena, there's a playhouse.
   b. Most children like to play house.
2. a. About that I know nothing and care less.
   b. He's always a little careless.
3. a. Try to keep the street cleaner.
   b. This town needs a street-cleaner.
4. a. In Africa, the British have a strong hold.
   b. Gibraltar is a stronghold.
5. a. Now that John's here, we are *all* ready.
   b. We've been there already.

E. Outside of class your instructor will mark the intonation patterns of this passage and record the material following his own markings. He will then play the recording several times, sentence by sentence, for the class. Listen to his intonation line and try to mark the passage so as to show what his patterns were. He will probably use some patterns with which you are not yet familiar, but don't try to analyze these. The exercise is intended merely to help you develop your ability to hear intonation.

Passage to be Marked

1. I usually get up early. 2. It takes me about half an hour to brush my teeth, shave, and get ready to leave the house. 3. On Tuesdays and Thursdays I sometimes take a swim before breakfast. 4. Do you like to swim? 5. There's nothing else like it to start the day off right. 6. What else would give you such an appetite?

F. The material below is to be prepared for reading and then to be read.

1. There are fifteen sentences of various kinds in the exercise. All but three of these would normally be pronounced with rising-falling intonation. Try to find the three exceptions, and eliminate them.
   a. Do you recall the types of sentence in which rising-falling intonation is normally used?

2. Mark the sentence-stresses of the twelve sentences which remain.
   a. *Milk-shake machine* (in Sentence 5) and *napkin holder* (9) are cases of two nouns used together. Position of stress?

b. Are *cleaned up* (4), *pick out* (8), and *look at* (1) two-word verbs? Position of stress?
c. Where would it be best to stress *fifteen* (13)?

3. Mark the intonation of each sentence. First, put the *high* note in its proper place; then fill in the rest of the rising-falling pattern. Everything which precedes the high note may be marked as *normal*.
    a. Which sentences end in inflections? How do you recognize them?

Sentences to be Marked

1. Look at the people.

2. What shall we order?

3. Where is the waiter?

4. He hasn't cleaned up the table.

5. He's there by the milk-shake machine.

6. Do you know what you want?

7. May I see the menu?

8. What shall I pick out?

9. Pass me the napkin holder.

10. We'd better order very soon.

11. Will you have an appetizer?

12. We don't have much time.

13. We have fifteen minutes.

14. I'll have the regular dinner.

15. Bring us our coffee later.

G. Transcribe in phonetic symbols Sentences 1, 3, 6, 9, 10, 13, and 15 of the preceding exercise. After you have made your transcription, your instructor will read the sentences and perhaps transcribe the exercise in class, so that you can check your work. Practice reading your corrected version.

H. Outside of class, do as much reading aloud as you can, concentrating your attention on obscuring the proper vowels in unstressed words of one syllable.

LESSON VI

Rising Intonation

I. The Use of Rising Intonation

In the preceding lesson, we studied rising-falling intonation as one of the two most important types used at the end of sentences. The second such type is rising intonation.

IN ENGLISH, RISING INTONATION IS NORMALLY USED AT THE END OF QUESTIONS WHICH DO NOT BEGIN WITH AN INTERROGATIVE WORD (that is to say, questions which may be answered merely by yes or no).

> Are you ready?   Will you read it for me?

The voice normally goes up to a high note *on the last sentence-stress*, just as in the rising-falling pattern. The difference between the two lies in the fact that, in rising intonation, the syllables which follow the rise are pronounced on the high note too.

> Does he expect to take a blanket with him?

When we leave our voice high at the end of a sentence, we arouse in the listener a feeling of incompleteness, in contrast to the sense of completeness aroused by a lowered voice. Rising intonation suggests that something further must be said, either by the speaker or by the hearer.

Any statement may be made into a question by the use of rising intonation alone, without changing the words themselves in any way:

> It's time for the class to end.   (statement)

It's time for the class to end?   (question)

II. Non-Final Intonation.

What has been said up to this point applies to the raising or lowering of the voice *at the end of a sentence*, where correct intonation is most necessary and easiest to predict. There is less that is definite to be said about the intonation of that part of the sentence which precedes the last important word. *Non-final intonation may vary widely from speaker to speaker*, with little corresponding variation in meaning.

In any sentence we may pronounce on a note higher than normal the stressed syllable of any word or words to which we want to call the special attention of the listener. These may be specially stressed function words (see Lesson IV, end of Section II, paragraph beginning "The usual rhythm units . . . ") or content words.

What are you doing here?   (Note *you*.)

There are lots of cigarettes in the box.   (Note *lots*.)

He has an unusual number of friends.   (Note *unusual*.)

With particular frequency special attention is thus called to *demonstrative* and *interrogative* words:

I don't think that is a good idea.

What do you want with a car?

In *contrasts* and *comparisons*, special attention is called to *both* ideas being compared or contrasted. If both ideas are included in a single thought group, the first one will be given a non-final high note.

Betty dances better than I do.

The new team is as good as the old one.

Note that in this construction we normally use the unstressed function words *do* or *one* in the second part of the contrast, rather than repeating the content words, *dances, team,* or whatever they may be.

If a sentence is divided by pauses into two or more *thought groups,* each thought group has its own separate intonation pattern. When the speaker comes to finish the first thought group, he may do one of three things:

1. End the group with the rising-falling pattern -- up to a high note, then down to a low one. This is done before a long pause such as might be marked by a colon(:) or semicolon(;).

    Let me tell you this: //it can't be done.

    I don't want to go; //it's dangerous.

    I say he can; //he says he can't.

2. End the group by a high note on its final stress, then a return to normal. This is done when the speaker wishes to suggest that what follows is connected with what he has just said.

    I think I know, //but I won't tell.

    If you want me to, //I'll call her.

3. End the group with the rising pattern. This occurs, in general, whenever the speaker wishes to create suspense.

    When I come back//I'll give you a present.

If you wánt to léarn chemistry.//

you'll háve to wŏrk.

It should be clearly understood that the choice between these three non-final patterns usually depends more on *the attitude of the speaker* than on the grammatical structure and meaning of the sentence. It is often impossible to say that, before a non-final pause, one type of intonation is "right" and all others "wrong". As far as grammar and logic are concerned, the last example above might just as well be:

If you wánt to léarn chemistry.//

you'll háve to wŏrk.

Certain special constructions, however, are spoken with the same intonation regularly enough to justify their being called to the student's attention. These are:

    1. *Alternatives with "or."* Rising intonation is used for all except the final alternative; the latter is given the rising-falling pattern. The speaker thus emphasizes the contrast between the various possible choices.

You can dó it in writing //or orally.

We éat at a drúgstore, //a cafetéria,//

or a restaurant.

This special pattern is used even if the alternatives are in a question which does not begin with an interrogative word, a type of sentence at the end of which rising intonation would normally be expected (see Section I of this lesson).

Will you have sugar // or lemon?

Do you drive a Ford, // a Plymouth, //

or a Chevrolet?

2. *Series with "and"*. The same pattern as for alternatives: rising intonation on all members of the series except the last; rising-falling intonation on the last member.

I went to the bank // and the post office.

He speaks English, // Italian, // and French.

3. *Direct address*. Rising intonation is used for names (or words substituted for names) and titles addressed directly to the person to whom one is speaking. These may come at the end of the sentence or elsewhere, and do not affect the intonation of the rest of the sentence.

My friend, // I'm glad to see you.

How are you feeling, // Mister Roberts?

4. *Reiterative formulas*, such as "aren't you," "will he." These show clearly the essential difference between rising-falling and rising intonation. If the reiterative formula is pronounced with the rising-falling pattern,

You're hungry, // aren't you?

the whole sentence is to be interpreted as a statement of fact, and indicates that the speaker is confident that the hearer will agree that he is hungry. When the formula is pronounced with the *rising* pattern,

You're hungry. //aren't you?

the sentence is a *genuine question*, which means that the speaker is not sure whether or not the hearer is hungry, and that the latter is asked to confirm or deny the idea, to answer *yes* or *no*. Note that the intonation of the part of the sentence which precedes the formula is not affected by the addition of the latter; though in the examples above *you're hungry* is non-final, it has the same intonation that would be given it if it came at the end of the sentence.

III. When the High Note Does Not Coincide With the Last Sentence-Stress.

The last example given in the preceding section,

You're hungry. //aren't you?

shows us for the first time a case in which the high note does not coincide with the last sentence-stress (see the "rule" in Lesson V, at the beginning of Section II). This is because the reiterative formula is very short -- only two syllables long. In saying those two words, the voice must rise; in order that the upward movement may be quite clear, the first syllable is needed for the lower note, and the second syllable for the high one.

A number of syllables insufficient to permit developing the pattern normally is, then, one of the reasons for giving the high note to a syllable other than that which receives the last sentence-stress. This phenomenon may be observed in all four of the special constructions listed at the end of the preceding section:

Shall we paint it red, // purple, // or green?

(Alternatives, note *purple*.)

I'll have spinach,// carrots,// and potatoes.

(Series, note carrots.)

Come here,// William,// I want to speak to you.

(Direct address, note William.)

If, in one of these constructions, there is only one syllable on which to make the rising intonation heard, then the voice must move upward *within that syllable*, thus making a sort of upward inflection.

Is your name Tom, // Dick//, or Harry? (Note Dick.)

What are you looking for, // son? (Note son.)

A second reason for giving the final high note to a syllable other than that which receives the last sentence-stress may be *a desire to single out one word or idea for special attention*. We have already seen how special attention can cause the stressing of a normally unstressed function word (Lesson IV, end of Section II), and the use of a non-final high note (Section II of this lesson). Sometimes the logic of the situation demands that one word or idea be made more important than any other in the sentence or thought group. The question,"Will you drive to the office tomorrow?", is vague without special intonation. Just what is the speaker asking about? Does he mean, "Will *you* drive, rather than the *chauffeur*?" Does he mean, "Will you *drive*, rather than *walk*?" Does he mean, "Will you drive *to the office*, rather than *anywhere else*?" Or does he mean, "Will you drive *tomorrow*, rather than *some other time*?" In order to make his meaning clear, he needs a way to focus the question around one of the several ideas it contains.

Special attention can be focused on one of the words in a thought group by using only one high note, and by making the voice rise on the stressed syllable of the word the speaker wishes to single out, regardless of whether this is the last sentence-stress or not.

Will you drive to the office tomorrow? (rather than the chauffeur)

Will you drive to the office tomorrow?   (rather than walk)

Will you drive to the office tomorrow?   (rather than anywhere else)

Will you drive to the office tomorrow?   (rather than some other time)

Will you drive to the office tomorrow?   (no one idea singled out)

In the same way one idea can be singled out in a rising-falling pattern:

It's my brother who needs it   (rather than I).

The need for thus singling out one idea in a thought group arises regularly in:

1. *Making a question specific.*

   Was it you who did that?

   When do you hope to leave?

2. *Answering a specific question.*
   (Who took the new car?)

   I took the new car.

   (Did you take the new car, or leave it?)

   I took the new car.

   (Did you take the new car, or the old one?)

   I took the new car.

3. *Contradicting an idea expressed elsewhere or merely implied.*
   (He's not working hard.)

   Yes, he is working hard.

(Johnny will bring it to you.)

I wánt you to bríng it to me.

(Will you please bring it here?)

Jóhnny will bríng it to you.

I líke this récord.

But we do belíeve you.

IV. Other Types of Intonation.

There are many intonation patterns, other than those described in the last two lessons, which are at times used by native speakers of English. Thus, emotional emphasis may be expressed by the use of an unusually high note in rising-falling intonation:

Thát's térrible!

A question which does not begin with an interrogative word may be given an added meaning of irony if it is pronounced with rising-falling intonation, like a statement of fact:

Do I know him? (He's my brother!)

A recent authoritative work on the subject[1] describes thirty different "primary intonation contours." However, beyond the point reached in these two lessons, the principles become too complicated to be of much practical value to a foreign student of English, and depend largely on mood and point of view, rather than grammatical construction and logic.

The simple types we have studied are sufficient, at the beginning, for normal conversational purposes. With them you can say almost anything in a natural and understandable way. Become as familiar with them as possible, and for a while try to use them for everything you say in English. Then, little by little, you can add new contours -- you will probably do so instinctively —by imitation.

---

1. Kenneth L. Pike, *The Intonation of American English*, Ann Arbor, University of Michigan Press, 1946.

Above all, do not make the mistake of thinking that all the various types of intonation you have been accustomed to using in your own language will have the same meaning if you transfer them to English. Many of your "intonation contours" do not exist in English, and others have entirely different meanings.

V. Exercises.

A. Read the following exercise silently to make sure you understand the meaning of each sentence. Then pronounce each group of sentences several times, so as to accustom yourself to the various intonation patterns. Your instructor will try to see that you do not neglect to blend your words together smoothly.

1. du yu rimémbər mi?

2. ɪz ðɛər ə rŭm for əs?

3. yu həv nə́θɪŋ t∫ípər?

4. wɪəl yu bí hɪər lóŋ?

5. ər yu góɪŋ tə sté wɪθ əs?

6. ər yu lívɪŋ ɪn ðɪs hotɛ́əl?

7. ɪz ðǽt dʒɪn óvər ðɛər?

8. ɪz ðɪs hwɛər yu ít?

9. wɪəl yu mít əs ðɪs ívnɪŋ?

10. ɪz ðə sɛ́kənd flór tu ló for yú?

11. yú láɪk ɪt æz wɛ́əl æz ɑ́ɪ du.

12. ðə ˈbrɛkfəsts ər ˈbɛtər ðæn ðə ˈdɪnərz.

13. ðɪs ˈrum ɪz mór ɪkspɛ́nsɪv ðæn ˈðæt wən.

14. du yu nó ˈdʒán, // ˈáfər?

15. dont ðe ˈɔl se so, // ˈdʒán?

16. hau ˈɑr yu, // ˈmɪstər ˈsmɪθ?

17. wɪəl sí yu ˈlétər, // ˈyáŋ ˈmæn.

18. ˈaɪm glǽd tə ˈmit yu, // ˈmɪsɪz ˈsmɪθ?

19. ˈhwɑt ər yu ˈdúɪŋ ˈhɪ́ər, // ˈwɪ́lyəm?

20. aɪ hav ˈmɛt yur ˈwaɪf, // ˈmɪstər ˈdʒǽksən.

21. maɪ ˈfrɛnd, // aɪ wánt tə ˈtsɛl yu sə́mθɪŋ.

22. ˈmɪstər ˈdʒǽksən, // ðɪs ɪz ˈmɪsɪz ˈsmɪθ.

23. yu wánt ə ˈbǽθ, // ˈdónt yu?

24. ɪt wɪəl bi ˈláɪər ˈhɪ́ər, // ˈwónt ɪt?

25. ˈðɛərz ə ˈplɛ́zənt ˈbriz, // ˈɪzənt ðɛər.

26. yu həv ə byútrfəl vyú,//hǽvənt yu.

27. ʃǽl wi mít hfər,//ɑr ɪn yúr rúm?

28. wʊd yu lɑ́ɪk ə dʌ́bəl bɛ́d,//ər twɪ́n bɛ́dz?

29. ɑɪ sɔ́ tʃɑ́rlz,//rɑ́bərt,//ən hǽrɪ.

30. wiəl bí hɪər mɑ́ndɪ,//tyúzdɪ,//ən wɛ́nzdɪ.

31. ɑɪ kən gɪv yu wən æt fɑ́ɪv,//sɪ́ks,//
    ər sɛ́vən dɑ́lərz.

32. dónt kʌ́m ərlɪ;//kʌ́m æt ʃɛ́t.

33. ɑɪ sé wi dú;//hí sɛ́z wi dónt.

34. ðɪ́s wən ɪz fɑ́ɪv;//ðǽt wən ɪz sɪ́ks.

35. ɪf yu wɪ́ʃ,//ɑɪ sɛ́rv yu nɑ́ʊ.

36. æz yu sɛ́d,//ɪts ə vɛ́rɪ nɑ́ɪs plɛ́s.

37. ɪn ə mɪ́nɪt,//ɑɪ hæv ə sərprɑ́ɪz for yu.

38. ɑɪ lʊ́kt dɑ́ʊn,//ən ðɛ́ər wəz ə dɑ́lər bɪ́əl.

39. ɪts ənbɪlívəbəl!

40. hwɑt ə byútɪfəl dś!

41. hwɑt ə stréndʒ sɛnséʃən!

42. ɑɪ névər só sɛ́tʃ ə gə́rl!

B. In order to improve your ability to control the ups and downs of your voice, to hear and produce an intonation pattern, it is suggested that a recording of Exercise A be made in class. As many students as possible should record groups of sentences, and these latter be played back to the class immediately. The students will try to detect any failure to reproduce the pattern.

C. Read each of these sentences, first as a statement, then as a question, using only intonation to show the difference (see Section I of this lesson):

1. The story begins long ago.
2. They were riding in an old car.
3. The car began to cross the river.
4. The bridge had been washed away.
5. The children were in the back seat.
6. They were talking at the top of their voice.
7. No one could hear anything.
8. One of the children fell out.

D. Pronounce each of the following questions in two ways: first, as if you were really asking for information; then, as if you knew the hearer would agree with you. After each reading of each sentence, another student should try to make the response which your intonation shows you expect of him. (See the end of Section II in this lesson.)

1. It's a nice day, isn't it?
2. You don't think it will rain, do you?
3. It doesn't rain here in August, does it?
4. The nights are always cool, aren't they?
5. You can count on good weather in October, can't you?

6. The rainy season doesn't begin until winter, does it?
7. There's some fog then too, isn't there?
8. The mornings are warmer than the afternoons.

E. 1. By using the proper intonation, make this sentence, *I put my black coat away*, serve as an answer to each of the following questions (see Section III of this lesson):

   a. What did you put away?
   b. Where did you put your black coat?
   c. Did the maid put your black coat away for you?
   d. What coat did you put away?
   e. Whose black coat did you put away?

2. Formulate a question which might result in each of the following answers; the intonation of the questions is important.

   a. She lost her pocketbook.

   b. She lost her pocketbook.

   c. She lost her pocketbook.

   d. She lost her pocketbook.

3. Authors do not usually know anything about the theory of intonation, yet they frequently indicate by putting a word in italics that their sentences should be read with a certain intonation pattern. The lines below are taken from recent plays. How do you think the author intended them to be spoken?

   a. They don't want *me*.
   b. *That's* a train trip for you.
   c. I don't know *what* I'm going to do.
   d. *Everybody* graduated this year.
   e. We *don't* have to show you.

F. 1. The sentences below are to be marked for rhythm and intonation, and then read. A systematic way of analyzing material for this purpose is to:

   a Mark all sentence-stresses. (In Part 1 of this exercise, all words may be stressed

normally: there are no specially stressed function words.)
b. Divide into thought groups by placing a // at pauses. Be sure to mark as separate thought groups all 1) alternatives, 2) parts of a series, 3) words used in direct address, and 4) reiterative formulas.
c. Mark the intonation of each group. First, locate the final high note or rise. (In Part 1 of this exercise, this may in all cases coincide with the last sentence-stress.) Second, determine whether the pattern should be rising-falling or rising, by deciding whether the group is a statement, command, question with interrogative word, question without interrogative word, non-final group, or one of the special constructions listed under b above. Third, mark the intonation line from the final high note to the end of the group, distinguishing between shifts and inflections. Fourth, decide whether or not you wish to give a high note to any non-final sentence-stresses, and mark such notes. Lastly, draw a line just under the rest of the group, indicating normal pitch.

Sentences to Analyze

a. Good morning, teacher. How are you feeling?

b. If it should rain, we'll call off the whole thing.

c. You'll agree that it's the truth, won't you?

d. Is the test on Monday or Tuesday?

e. We study composition, pronunciation,

and grammar.

   f. There are two ways of doing it: by kindness, or by threats.

   g. He translates from English to French, and from French to English.

   h. Which syllable is accented?

   i. Miss Sarmenta, will you open the door?

   j. Do you speak better than you read, or read better than you speak?

2. The sentences below are to be treated just like those above. However, this second part of the exercise includes a few cases of specially stressed function words (see Lesson IV, end of Section II), and of final high notes which do not coincide with the last sentence-stress (see Section III of this lesson).

   a. It's not a large book; it's a very small one.

   b. The class begins at four, and ends at five.

c. A student may be good, bad, or indifferent.

d. Do you want me, or him?

e. Does he live on the left-hand side of the street?

f. He lives on the right-hand side.

G. Transcribe the following paragraph in phonetic symbols; then mark sentence-stresses, pauses, and intonation. After you have completed your analysis, your instructor will read the sentences, so that you can check your work with his pronunciation. It is not expected that each member of the class will mark the paragraph in exactly the same way. Finally, practice reading your corrected transcription.

"1. Yes dear, I know what I'm to bring home: bread, butter, and cheese. 2. It's written down here in my notebook, so I won't forget it. 3. Shall I get a pound of butter, or half a pound? 4. What kind of butter do you want? 5. As for me, I like local butter. 6. But I'm sure you want Wisconsin butter, don't you."

H. Outside of class, read aloud several pages of simple conversational material (a modern play, if possible), concentrating your attention on the intonation of questions which begin with an interrogative word.

LESSON VII

Classification of Consonants; the Endings -s and -ed

I. Voiced and Voiceless Sounds.

An important way in which one speech sound may differ from another is in voicing or the lack of it. We say that a sound is *voiced* if our vocal cords vibrate as we pronounce it; a sound is *voiceless* if it is pronounced *without such vibration*. Press your thumb and forefinger lightly against the sides of your larynx (the central part of your throat, where sounds are made); then pronounce [Z] and [S] alternately. You should be able to feel the vibration of the vocal cords as you say [Z], and notice no vibration as you say [S]. In other words, [Z] is a voiced sound and [S] is voiceless.

Now try pronouncing [ʃ] and [ʒ]. Which of the two sounds is voiced?

Another means of distinguishing the two types is to stop your ears as you pronounce the sounds aloud. In the case of voiced sounds, you should then be able to hear clearly the vibration of the vocal cords. You will hear nothing, except perhaps the rushing of air, as you say the voiceless sounds.

The Voiced Consonants Are:

b	m	ð	z
d	n	v	ʒ
g	ŋ	w	dʒ
l	r	y	

The Voiceless Consonants Are:

f	s	hw
h	ʃ	tʃ
k	t	
p	θ	

[69]

All Vowel Sounds Are Voiced.

Do not try to memorize the above lists. It is much better to pronounce all the sounds to yourself, with fingers on throat or in ears, until you can tell instantly whether each one is voiced or voiceless.

You may have noticed that there are a number of pairs of consonants -- such as [s] and [z], [ʃ] and [ʒ] -- which seem to be very much alike except that one is voiced and the other voiceless. [b] and [p] form another such pair: both sounds are made in the same place, between the lips, and in the same manner, by closing the lips then opening them to let the air escape explosively; but [b] is pronounced with vibration of the vocal cords, and [p] without vibration. We may say that [b] is the voiced counterpart of [p]. How many more such pairs can you discover?

Pronounce a prolonged [v]. In the middle of the sound, without interrupting the flow of air through your mouth, make your vocal cords stop vibrating. What sound is left? What is the voiceless counterpart of [v]?

What happens if you stop the vibration of the vocal cords while pronouncing [m]? We may say, then, that [m] has no voiceless counterpart. The same is true of [l], [n], [ŋ], [r], [w], and [y]. On the other hand, there are no voiced sounds corresponding to [h] and [hw].

This leaves the following pairs:

b/p   ð/θ   ʒ/ʃ
d/t   v/f   dʒ/tʃ
g/k   z/s

[b] and [p] may be regarded as two parts of the same sound; so may [d] and [t], [g] and [k], etc. In each case, the first symbol represents the voiced half of the sound, the second symbol the voiceless half.

Since there is so little difference between [z] and [s], for example, it is extremely easy to make the error of pronouncing one in place of the other. In some languages, such as German, there are very few final voiced consonants. When speaking English, a person whose first language was German will therefore have a strong tendency to unvoice final consonants whenever possible. If he sees the word *bed*, he may think he pronounces it as [bɛd], but to an American it will probably seem that he says [bɛt̪]. We shall speak of the problem again in later lessons.

II. Stops and Continuants, Sibilants.

It is sometimes useful to classify consonants in a second way, as *stops* or *continuants*. A continuant is a sound -- like [m] -- which may be prolonged indefinitely, as long as the speaker has breath to pronounce it. A stop must be pronounced instantaneously, and cannot be held -- like [t].

Is [n] a stop or a continuant? What is [s]? [k]? [b]? [f]?

Among the continuants, a group of four consonants are known as sibilants, because of the hissing sound with which they are pronounced. These are [z], [s], [ʒ], and [ʃ]. Note that these four make up two voiced-voiceless pairs: [z/s] and [ʒ/ʃ]. The classification of sibilant is significant, as we shall see shortly, in determining the pronunciation of the ending -s, which is so frequently used in English.

III. Point of Articulation.

We shall also need to be able to classify consonants in one other way, as to their *point of articulation*, or the place in the mouth where they are pronounced. Thus [p] is pronounced between the lips, and for [g] the back of the tongue is pressed against the roof of the mouth.

If we begin at the front of the mouth and work back, we shall find first a group of three sounds made with *the lips*. Can you identify the three without consulting the list below? They are a voiced stop, a voiceless stop, and a voiced continuant.

Between *the upper teeth and the lower lip*, we make two English sounds: a voiced continuant and a voiceless one. What are they?

By inserting the tongue *between the teeth* we make another pair of continuants.

By touching the tip of the tongue to *the tooth ridge* (just behind the upper teeth), we make four sounds: a voiced stop, a voiceless stop, and two voiced continuants. In several languages other than English, these same sounds are pronounced with the tongue tip touching the upper teeth themselves.

By allowing the air to escape through *a narrow*

passage between the tongue and the tooth ridge, we form four continuants, two of which are voiced and two voiceless.

Pressing the back of the tongue against the roof of the mouth, we form a voiced stop, a voiceless stop, and a continuant.

Consult the following table only when you have made a careful attempt to discover for yourself the various consonant sounds described above.

Points of Articulation

LIPS: b,p,m
UPPER TEETH AND LOWER LIPS: v,f
BETWEEN TEETH: ð,θ
TOOTH RIDGE: d,t,n,l
PASSAGE BETWEEN TONGUE AND TOOTH RIDGE: z, s, ʒ, ʃ

ROOF OF MOUTH: g,k,ŋ

The points of articulation of the other consonants — [h], [y], [r], [w], [hw], [tʃ], and [dʒ] — will be described in later sections devoted specially to those sounds.

IV. Pronunciation of -ed.

The ending -ed, added to regular English verbs as a sign of the past tense and past participle forms, has three different pronunciations: [t] as in *wished* [wɪʃt], [d] as in *failed* [feəld], and [ɪd] as in *needed* [nɪdɪd].

The sound the ending will have in any given word is determined by a very simple phonetic principle: when two consonants are pronounced together, as [r] and [d] in *cared* [kɛərd], it is difficult to voice one and leave the other voiceless, and easy to voice both or leave both voiceless. Therefore, the ending -ed is pronounced [d] after a voiced sound, and [t] after a voiceless sound. You will remember that [d] and [t] are the two halves of a voiced-voiceless pair; in phonetic terms, this pair [d/t] is the sign of the past tense and past participle.

How would the ending -ed be pronounced after a vowel? Remember that all vowels are voiced.

Let us suppose now that we wish to add the sound [d] or [t] to a word which already ends in one of those two sounds, in other words, to add [d/t] to [d/t]. It is almost impossible to do so without inserting some sort of a vowel sound between the two consonants. Because vowels are voiced, the insertion of a vowel here means that the final d will be pronounced as [d] rather than [t]. In other words, after t or d the ending -ed is pronounced as a separate syllable, [ɪd].

To sum up, we may say that

THE ENDING -ED IS PRONOUNCED:
1. [d] AFTER ALL VOICED CONSONANTS EXCEPT [d], AND AFTER ALL VOWEL SOUNDS.
   planned [plænd] judged [dʒədʒd] played [pled]
2. [t] AFTER ALL VOICELESS CONSONANTS EXCEPT [t].
   rocked [rakt] kissed [kɪst] ripped [rɪpt]
3. AS A SEPARATE SYLLABLE, [ɪd], AFTER [d/t].
   protected [prətéktɪd]   intended [ɪnténdɪd]

The most common errors which result from failure to observe the above principles are:
1. The pronunciation of -ed as a separate syllable after consonants other than [d] or [t].
   robbed as [rábɪd], instead of [rabd]
   thanked as [θǽŋkɪd], instead of [θæŋkt]
2. The pronunciation of -ed as [t] after [l], [r], or a vowel.
   dared as [dɛərt], instead of [dɛərd].
   killed as [kɪəlt], instead of [kɪəld].
3. Apparent omission of the entire ending.
   answered as [ǽnsər], instead of [ǽnsərd].

There is only one type of exception to these rules, a group of *adjectives* which end in -ed, and therefore look like verbs: *ragged, wretched*, etc. Contrary to the principles outlined above, the ending of these words is pronounced as a separate syllable, [ɪd]: [rǽgɪd], [rɛ́tʃɪd].

An *aged* [édʒɪd] minister.
The *blessed* [blésɪd] virgin.
   (but
The Pope *blessed* [blɛst] the crowd).
A *dogged* [dɔ́gɪd] determination.
A *naked* [nékɪd] child.
A *ragged* [rǽgɪd] coat.
The *rugged* [rǽgɪd] rock.
A *two-legged* [túlégɪd] animal.
A *wicked* [wɪ́kɪd] idea.
A *wretched* [rɛ́tʃɪd] day.

V. Pronunciation of -s.

In English, to make a noun plural or possessive, or to put a verb in the third person singular form of the present tense, we add [z/s] to the end of the word. This ending is spelled in several different ways: -s (two hours, he says), -es (several churches, she kisses), -'s (a moment's time), or -s' (the grocers' prices). However it may be spelled, the ending is pronounced, according to strict phonetic principles, in one of three ways: [z], [s], or [ɪz]. The principles are the same as those which determine the pronunciation of -ed. Can you formulate them for yourself?

THE ENDING -S (-ES, -'S, or -S') IS PRONOUNCED:

1. [z] AFTER ALL VOICED CONSONANTS EXCEPT [z] AND [ʒ], AND AFTER ALL VOWEL SOUNDS.

    games [gemz]   calls [kɔlz]   shows [ʃoz]

2. [s] AFTER ALL VOICELESS CONSONANTS EXCEPT [s] AND [ʃ].

    Jack's [dʒæks]   grants [grænts]   wraps [ræps]

3. AS A SEPARATE SYLLABLE, [ɪz], AFTER A SIBILANT ([z/s] OR [ʒ/ʃ]).

    houses [hɑuzɪz]   George's [dʒɔrdʒɪz]   foxes [fɑksɪz]

The above rules apply only when s is added to a word as an ending. If the final s is a part of the basic word itself, as in as, yes, etc., there is no logical way to decide whether it will be pronounced [s] or [z]. Here is a list of the most common such words:

[z]	[s]
as [æz]	this [ðɪs]
has [hæz] or [həz]	thus [ðəs]
his [hɪz]	us [əs]
is [ɪz]	yes [yɛs]
was [wɑz] or [wəz]	

VI. Exercises.

A. Are the following sounds voiced or voiceless? Divide them into two lists, and compare your results with the tables in Section I of this lesson:

1. f	5. ʒ	9. n	13. tʃ	17. dʒ	21. hw	25. i
2. s	6. z	10. r	14. h	18. k	22. b	26. y
3. ʃ	7. m	11. ŋ	15. t	19. d	23. w	27. ð
4. v	8. l	12. a	16. e	20. p	24. θ	28. g

American English Pronunciation 75

B. 1. What is the voiced counterpart of: ʃ, f, k, tʃ, θ, p, s, t?
   2. How would a person with a "German accent" probably pronounce the underscored letters in this sentence (see Section I): "His language shows that he is glad to have the job and the big salary that goes with it"?

C. Classify the following sounds as *voiced* or *voiceless*, *stop* or *continuant*, and give the point of articulation of each. For example, [d] is a voiced stop, made with the tongue against the tooth ridge.

   1. v   4. ʃ   7. l   10. m   13. ŋ   16. s
   2. b   5. ð   8. p   11. d   14. g   17. k
   3. n   6. t   9. θ   12. ʒ   15. f   18. z

D. Suppose a student from Latin America pronounces very incorrectly, [bɛrɪ] instead of [vɛrɪ]. Keeping in mind what you know about points of articulation, what would you tell him to do with his lips, teeth, etc., in order to change [b] to [v]? How would you help a French student to say *think* as [θɪŋk] instead of [sɪŋk]? *Those* as [ðoz] instead of [zoz]? A Chinese student to pronounce *man* as [mæn] instead of [mæŋ]? A German student to pronounce *that* as [ðæt] instead of [dæt]? A Scandinavian to say *thanks* as [θæŋks] instead of [tæŋks]?

E. Pronounce each of these words, and write the phonetic symbol which represents the sound you gave to the ending. Then, in each case, explain why the ending is pronounced as it is.

   1. added   7. showed   13. dropped   19. followed
   2. armed   8. lasted   14. changed   20. watched
   3. answered   9. caused   15. laughed   21. robbed
   4. boxed   10. asked   16. learned   22. believed
   5. wished   11. lighted   17. crossed   23. wicked
   6. aired   12. wretched   18. minded   24. longed
                                                   25. called

   26. belongs   32. blesses   38. is   44. cars
   27. bees   33. branches   39. arrives   45. armies
   28. ages   34. breaks   40. chances   46. allows
   29. acts   35. attends   41. us   47. chiefs
   30. bottoms   36. articles   42. appears   48. America's
   31. bags   37. caps   43. fixes   49. animals
                                                   50. bridges

F. On page 73 of this lesson, you will find listed the three most common types of error made in pronouncing -*ed*. The errors made in pronouncing the ending

-s, -es, etc., are fundamentally the same as items 2 and 3 on this list. Can you restate these two items in terms of -s, and give examples?

G. Where would the high note or notes of the intonation pattern fall in the sentences below? In each of them the special attention of the hearer should be focused on one or two ideas, because of a comparison, contrast, contradiction, or a desire to make a question or an answer specific. (See Lesson VI, Section II, and the last part of Section III.) The sentences make up a connected passage, and should be considered in the light of what precedes and follows. Underline the syllables on which attention is to be focused, and then read the exercise with the proper intonation.

1. Her composition is better than mine.
2. Isn't his still better?
3. No, I have a higher grade than he has.
4. What grade did Robert get?
5. He got an "A."
6. No, he didn't get an "A."
7. He got "C" on his paper.
8. On the one he handed in this afternoon, or the one he handed in yesterday afternoon?
9. The one he handed in this afternoon.
10. What was the subject of the paper?

H. The passage which follows has been transcribed in phonetic symbols, and marked for rhythm and intonation as an American might speak it. In other words, almost everything possible has been done so that your eye may help your ear and speech organs in pronouncing it. Read it several times, concentrating successively on 1) the sound of the symbols, 2) the regular return of sentence-stresses, 3) the intonation patterns, 4) combining all these elements. (If there is enough class time available, this exercise might well be recorded.)

1. wɔ́ltər stɑ́pt ðə kɑ́r //ɪn frʌ́nt əv ðə bfəldɪŋ,

   hwɛər hɪz waɪf wʌ́nt tə hǽv hər hɛər dʌ́n.

2. hwaɪl aɪm hǽvɪŋ maɪ hɛər dʌ́n, //rɪmɛ́mbər,

tə gét ðóz óvərʃuz,"// ʃi séd. 3. "ɑɪ dont nɪd

óvərʃuz."// séd wóltər. 4. ʃi pút hər mɪtənər bǽk

ɪntu hər bǽg. 5. "wiv dɪskə́st ól ðǽt,"// ʃi séd

gétɪŋ áut əv ðə kɑ́r. 6. "yu ɑrnt ə yə́ŋ mǽn ɛ́nɪ

lɔ́ŋgər." 7. "hi méd ðə mótər rə́n fǽstər.

8. "hwɑɪ dont yu wɛ́ər yur glə́vz?" ʃi ǽskt.

9. "həv yu lɔ́st yur glə́vz?" 10. wóltər rítʃt ɪn,

ə pɑ́kɪt // ən brɔ́t áut ðə glə́vz. 11. hi pút ðəm

ɔ́n.// bət ǽftər ʃi hæd tə́rnd ən gɔ́n ɪntu ðə

ɔ́fəldɪŋ // ən hi hæd drívən ɔ́n tə ə réd lɑ́ɪt.//

hi túk ðəm ɔ́f əgén.

(Adapted from the story, "The Secret Life
of Walter Mitty" by James Thurber, originally
published in *The New Yorker*.)

I. Read aloud several pages from a book you are
studying, concentrating your attention on the
pronunciation of the endings -s and -ed.

LESSON VIII

Initial and Final Consonants

I. The Aspiration of Initial Consonants.

In Lesson VII we considered the eight pairs of consonants: [b/p], [d/t], [g/k], [ð/θ], [v/f], [z/s], [ʒ/ʃ], and [dʒ/tʃ]. It was pointed out that, in each of these pairs, the first sound is very similar to the second, except that the one is voiced and the other is voiceless. The *chief difference*, then, between two words such as *big* [bɪg] and *pig* [pɪg], is that the initial consonant of *big* is pronounced with vibration of the vocal cords, and the initial consonant of *pig* without vibration.

However, that is not the only difference. Both [b] and [p] are stops, which means that they cannot be prolonged for more than a very short time. They are frequently pronounced so rapidly that it would be very difficult for the hearer to tell whether the vocal cords had vibrated or not. Possibly in an effort to make it easier to distinguish between words like *big* and *pig*, speakers of English have developed a secondary type of difference between initial voiced and voiceless consonants. The [p] of *pig* is pronounced with a little puff of air, or -- in more technical words -- the initial [p] is aspirated. When we say the [b] of *big*, no such puff of air enters into the sound.

When they come at the beginning of a word, all other voiceless consonants are aspirated, just as [p] is. This principle may be stated in the form of a rule:

VOICELESS CONSONANTS ARE ASPIRATED AT THE BEGINNING OF A WORD.

It may help you to remember the principle if you think of it this way: at the beginning of a word, a consonant is pronounced either with a puff of air (aspirated) or with vibration of the vocal cords (voiced).

In many other languages, initial voiceless conso-

nants are not regularly aspirated, and people who
learned one of these languages first usually find it
hard to aspirate properly in English. For example, a
German student may seem to say, "I am so ([zo] instead
of [so]) tired." This pronunciation may lead to misunderstanding, and is certain to be noticed as an element of "foreign accent". The student could correct his
mispronunciation by forming the first letter of so with
more sound of air escaping through his teeth and without vibration of the vocal cords.

When we are using phonetic symbols and feel that
it is important to show that a consonant is aspirated,
we write a small h above the line after the symbol:
time [tʰaɪm].

Medial consonants -- those which occur within a
word, after the first vowel sound and before the last--
are distinguished in much the same way as initial ones.
When voiced, they are not aspirated; when voiceless,
they are aspirated, though usually not so strongly as
initial consonants: safer [séfʰər], saver [sévər];
meeker [mɪ́kʰər], meager [mɪ́gər].

An exception among medial consonants is a special
type of [t] -- one which occurs between voiced sounds,
usually vowels, and does not stand at the beginning of
a stressed syllable: for example, the t's in atom and
hurting (but not the t in áfter, which stands between
a voiceless and a voiced sound; nor that of retell,
which stands at the beginning of a stressed syllable).
Many educated Americans appear to make no difference of
any sort between this type of [t] and a [d]. Atom [ǽtəm]
and Adam [ǽdəm] sound alike in their speech, and the
hearer must rely on the meaning of the sentence in
order to tell which is intended. It is probable, however, that many other speakers do make a very slight
difference between the two sounds. Until the facts are
better understood, perhaps the best advice that can be
given to a foreign student of English is to pronounce
this special medial [t] "somewhat like a [d]," and entirely without aspiration: butter [bə́tər], pretty
[prɪ́ti].

II. The Lengthening of Vowels Before Final Consonants.

Even more often than at the beginning of words,
voiced consonants are confused with their voiceless
counterparts, or vice versa, at the end of words: *I
live* ([lɪf] instead of [lɪv]) *in California*, or *Who was
it?* ([was] instead of [waz]) In the speech of students
of English, this type of error is probably more frequent than any other type, with the exception of the

failure to give unstressed vowels their normal sound of [ə] or [ɪ].

In doing the exercises of Lesson VII, you may have had great difficulty making a word like years sound like [yɪərz̠] instead of [yɪərs̠], even though you knew the final sound should be voiced, and tried hard to make your vocal cords vibrate as you pronounced it. The fact is that voicing or the lack of it is not the only difference between the [s] and [z] sounds at the end of a word. Just as in the case of initial consonants, we do not rely on vibration of the vocal cords alone to distinguish a final voiced consonant from its voiceless counterpart.

There are at least three differences between the sound of bus [bəs̠] and that of buzz [bəz̠]. The first is, of course, that [z] is voiced, [s] voiceless. The second is that the vowel before [z] is lengthened: it usually takes almost twice as long to say buzz as to say bus. The third difference will be discussed in Section III of this lesson.

If we wish to show by a phonetic symbol that a sound is lengthened, we place the symbol [ː] after it: buzz [bəːz].

The second difference mentioned above between final [s] and [z] also serves at the end of words to distinguish all other voiced consonants from their voiceless counterparts: bed [bɛːd] takes longer to say than bet [bɛt], rib [rɪːb] longer than rip [rɪp], bag [bæːg] longer than back [bæk]. The rule is:

BEFORE A FINAL VOICED CONSONANT, STRESSED VOWELS ARE LENGTHENED.

If you will deliberately try to lengthen the vowel, it may be easier for you to make years sound like [yɪərz̠] rather than [yɪərs̠]. This lengthening will increase the tendency toward diphthongization which is noticeable in many stressed English vowels.

III. Aspiration at the End of Words.

The third difference between bus [bəs̠] and buzz [bəz̠] (or [yɪərs̠] and [yɪərz̠]) is that the [s] is pronounced with a great deal of aspiration, the [z] with very little. In other words, at the end of [bəs̠] a listener can hear very clearly the sound of air escaping through the teeth; at the end of [bəz̠] there is much less sound of escaping air.

To sum up: if you find it hard to make a word like

years sound like [yɪərz̠] instead of [yɪərs̠], the difficulty with [z] may be overcome by trying consciously to:
1. Make your vocal cords vibrate to the very end of the word.
2. Lengthen the final vowel.
3. Allow very little sound of escaping air.

The aspiration which helps distinguish [s] at the end of a word, however, is *not* typical of all other voiceless consonants in the same position. Usually it is heard only with final voiceless *continuants* ([f̲], [s], [ʃ], and [θ]̲, not with final voiceless *stops* ([k̲], [p̲], and [t̲]):

safe [sef̲ʰ], save [seːv]
place [ples̲ʰ], plays [pleːz]
teeth [tiθ̲ʰ], teethe [tiːð]
but
lack [læk̲], lag [læːg]
rip [rɪp̲], rib [rɪːb]
debt [dɛt̲], dead [dɛːd]

The rule:

AT THE END OF A WORD, ONLY VOICELESS CONTINUANTS ARE STRONGLY ASPIRATED.

Many students from abroad do, however, try to aspirate final consonants which are not voiceless continuants. A Latin American may pronounce *I don't think so*, as [aɪ dontʰ θɪŋkʰ so]. The little puffs of air after [t] and [k] sound like extra syllables. In extreme cases, the student may even add an [ə] at the end of *don't* and *think* in order to aspirate the [t] and [k] more clearly: [aɪ dontʰə θɪŋkʰə so]. This, of course, completely destroys the natural rhythm of the sentence.

Normally, two movements are necessary for the production of a stop, such as [t], [k], or [p]. There is first a *closure*, or stopping of the outflow of air: for [t], the tongue tip presses against the tooth ridge; for [k], the back of the tongue rises and presses against the soft palate; for [p], the lips are closed. As soon as a little pressure has been built up, comes the second movement, the *release* of the air: for [t] the tongue tip leaves the tooth ridge; for [k], the back of the tongue falls away from the soft palate; for [p], the lips open. It is during this second movement that aspiration, the sound of escaping air, may be heard to a greater or lesser degree.

In conversational American English, there is such a powerful tendency to avoid the strong aspiration of final consonants (other than voiceless continuants), that at the end of a word we regularly pronounce only the first half of a stop. We make the closure, but allow our voice to die before the release. If we say, "A ship!" the sound ends while our lips are still pressed together for the [p], and the lips may not open again for some time. If we say, "You're right," we similarly avoid any "finishing sound" after [t]. It may seem to you that this would mean that the final [p] or [t] would simply not be heard. A native speaker of English, however, comes by long practice to be able to distinguish between final stops by the sound of their closure alone.

In general, the "finishing sound" (the puff of air, sometimes followed by an [ə], which is added at the end of a word) should be avoided in English. When, by the coming together of two words, a combination of consonants is produced which is quite hard to pronounce -- such as these three [ðiz θri], or first grade [fərst gred]--, there is a strong tendency for new speakers of English to separate the words and thus make the combination easier by inserting a finishing sound between them. This results in unnatural pronunciations such as [ðizhə θri], and [fərsthə gred]. The transition from [z] to [θ], and [t] to [g] must be made quickly and directly, so that no finishing sound can creep in (see Lesson IV, end of Section IV).

IV. Prothetic S.

A particularly difficult type of combination is one in which the second word begins with a prothetic s, an initial s followed immediately by another consonant: *United States* [yunditid stets], *great spirit* [gret spirit]. In many other languages, Spanish and Chinese for example, such combinations never occur. Students who learned those languages before English must resist very strongly the temptation to say [yunditid əstets] and [gret əspirit]. This type of mispronunciation can usually be avoided by taking care not to aspirate the sound with which the first word of the combination ends. Sometimes it is also helpful to think of the prothetic s as being a part of the preceding word; this would mean pronouncing the examples given above as though they were spelled *Uniteds Tates* and *greats pirit*.

V. Exercises.

A. Summarize this lesson by filling in the blanks below:

American English Pronunciation 83

TABLE OF DIFFERENCES

Between an initial (or medial) voiceless consonant and its voiced counterpart (Section I):

1. _____

2. _____

Examples: [_____] and [_____]
          [_____] and [_____]

Between a final voiceless stop and its voiced counterpart (Section II):

1. _____

2. _____

Examples: [_____] and [_____]
          [_____] and [_____]

Between a final voiceless continuant and its voiced counterpart (Sections II and III):

1. _____

2. _____

3. _____

Examples: [_____] and [_____]
          [_____] and [_____]

B. What advice (regarding aspiration, vowel length, and voicing) would you give a fellow student who made the following errors in pronunciation?:

1. Pronounced *had* as [hæt̪] instead of [hæd̪]
2. Pronounced *than* as [θæn] instead of [ðæn]
3. Pronounced *five* as [faɪf] instead of [faɪv]
4. Pronounced *log* as [lak] instead of [lag]
5. Pronounced *bus* as [bəz] instead of [bəs]
6. Pronounced *sing* as [zɪŋ] instead of [sɪŋ]
7. Pronounced *languages* as [længwɪtʃɪz] instead of [længwɪdʒɪz]

C. The following pairs of words differ only in that the first word of each pair contains a voiceless consonant, and the second contains the voiced counterpart of that consonant. Transcribe the words in phonetic symbols. Then, using the signs [ʰ] and [ː], mark the secondary difference or differences in each case. Finally, pronounce each series of words horizontally and vertically, taking great care to aspirate consonants and lengthen vowels as marked. Repeat this drill several times. It is best to use the same intonation for all words.

1. INITIAL (and medial) CONSONANTS
   a. chest [   ]   jest [   ]
   b. thigh [   ]   thy [   ]
   c. fine [   ]   vine [   ]
   d. sink [   ]   zinc [   ]
   e. stacker [   ]   stagger [   ]
   f. tie [   ]   die [   ]
   g. pour [   ]   bore [   ]

2. FINAL STOPS
   a. rack [   ]   rag [   ]
   b. rip [   ]   rib [   ]
   c. hit [   ]   hid [   ]
   d. peck [   ]   peg [   ]
   e. heart [   ]   hard [   ]
   f. ape [   ]   Abe [   ]

3. FINAL CONTINUANTS
   a. price [   ]   prize [   ]
   b. proof [   ]   prove [   ]
   c. teeth [   ]   teethe [   ]
   d. cease [   ]   sees [   ]
   e. strife [   ]   strive [   ]
   f. hiss [   ]   his [   ]

D. Read each of the sentences below twice, using word <u>a</u> in the first reading and word <u>b</u> in the second. Then read again and use either <u>a</u> or <u>b</u>, while another member of the class tries to identify in each case the word that you pronounced.

1. (a. *back*) (b. *pack*) Now I must go ―――――.
2. (a. *bear*) (b. *pear*) You can't eat a whole ―――――.
3. (a. *mob*) (b. *mop*) The leader kept the ――――― well in hand.
4. (a. *fast*) (b. *vast*) The patient has shown ――――― improvement.
5. (a. *feel*) (b. *veal*) He spoke on "The――――― of the Future".
6. (a. *few*) (b. *view*) We saw a ―――――on the hilltop.
7. (a. *safe*) (b. *save*) Nothing will make a careless man―――――.
8. (a. *cold*) (b. *gold*) Are you getting ――――― ?
9. (a. *cave*) (b. *gave*) Under great pressure they ―――――in.

10. (a. *back*) (b. *bag*) Put your coat on your _____.
11. (a. *dime*) (b. *time*) There's no _____ to lose.
12. (a. *bed*) (b. *bet*) I wouldn't jump that far on a _____.
13. (a. *dead*) (b. *debt*) We must never forget the _____.
14. (a. *feed*) (b. *feet*) He was off his _____.
15. (a. *grade*) (b. *great*) The child was put in a _____ school.
16. (a. *led*) (b. *let*) A traitor _____ the enemy in.
17. (a. *seal*) (b. *zeal*) His _____ is well known.
18. (a. *ice*) (b. *eyes*) You need good _____ to skate well.
19. (a. *loss*) (b. *laws*) You can't avoid the _____ of the land.
20. (a. *peace*) (b. *peas*) A meal without _____ is disappointing.
21. (a. *place*) (b. *plays*) Put yourself in his _____.
22. (a. *race*) (b. *raise*) I'll _____ you to the top.
23. (a. *bridges*) (b. *breeches*) Don't burn your _____.
24. (a. *ridge*) (b. *rich*) It was grown on _____ land.
25. (a. *ether*) (b. *either*) The doctor wouldn't give her _____.

Your teacher may wish to use the above drill as a test of your ability to distinguish between voiced and voiceless sounds when you hear them. If so, take a piece of paper and number the lines from 1 through 25. The teacher will read each sentence, inserting one of the two test words. You should decide which one he used and write a̲ or b̲ on your paper opposite the number of the sentence.

E. There follows an exercise which will give you a chance to work on the special type of medial [t] which is pronounced "somewhat like a [d]" (see end of Section I of this lesson).

1. Read these sentences, paying particular attention to the letters in italics:
   a. What's hur*t*ing you?
   b. She's ge*tt*ing the pota*t*oes.
   c. It's a pi*t*y you wai*t*ed so long.

       d. There's not enough wa_ter to ma_tter.
       e. Be_tty wan_ted to stay la_ter at the par_ty.
       f. They have be_tter bu_tter at Ralph's.
    2. Several members of the class should answer
       these questions by complete statements:
       a. How old do you think Be_tty Grable is
          (for_ty, thir_ty)?
       b. What girls do you think are pre_tty?
       c. What do you think of the a_tom bomb?
F. This drill is intended to give you practice in
   pronouncing difficult combinations of consonants without inserting a "finishing sound." Be
   particularly careful with the combinations
   which involve a prothetic s, as you pronounce
   the entire exercise several times. This material is well suited for individual laboratory
   work with a sound mirror or tape recorder.
    1. A large group of students graduates each
       spring.
    2. I heard that splendid speech you made last
       night.
    3. He changed his mind and lunched at the stu-
       dent cafeteria.
    4. They answered correctly, and the instructor
       thanked them.
    5. I request that all books be removed from the
       desks.
    6. He will need all his strength to catch the
       others.
    7. The next time you come we must speak Spanish.
    8. Someone's trying to turn my friends against
       me.
    9. Does she like this part of the United States?
   10. George nudged me and asked if we hadn't
       watched long enough.
   11. I wonder why that child acts so strangely.
   12. The baby has a big splinter in the skin of
       his finger.
   13. Thanksgiving comes the last Thursday in
       November.
   14. Do you expect to catch the next train?
   15. We'll have to risk using the old screens
       this year.
G. Let the members of the class ask one another
   questions about their amusements, living arrangements, etc. Each question and answer
   should include the name (or a substitute for
   the name) of the person addressed: "Have you
   seen a good movie lately, Natalie?", "Oh yes,

American English Pronunciation 87

Mr. Liebmann, I saw a wonderful one last night." The instructor should listen carefully to see that proper intonation is used for direct address. (See Lesson VI, end of Section II.)

H. The sentences which follow were chosen because they contain a great many final voiced consonants. First find and draw a circle around all these final voiced consonants, and be sure that you understand the meaning of the passage. Then pronounce each sentence several times. If your teacher feels that any of the final voiced consonants sound like their voiceless counterparts, see what you can do to improve the pronunciation by more vibration of the vocal cords cords, less aspiration, and a longer preceding vowel.

1. ðə plés ɪz kóld θríˈrívərz, // bɪkóz ɪts lóketɪd hwɛər ə lék ɪz fórmd baɪ θríˈstrímz.

2. ðɛər ar héndrədz əv kɪ́tɪdʒɪz ɔn ðə ʃórz əv ðə lék. 3. ðə hótɛlz sárv vɛ́rɪ gúd míəlz. 4. dʒémz həz spént fáɪv sémərz ðɛər // ən nóz évrɪbədɪ.

5. dyurɪŋ ðə dé hi swímz; // æt náɪt hi dénsɪz.

6. ðɪs yfər hi həz tékən twɛ́lv dífrənt gə́rlz tə pártɪz. 7. hi yúzɪz hɪz fáðərz kár // ən həz lə́rnd tə dráɪv ɪt kwáɪt wɛ́l. 8. ɪf hɪz fréndz ar bórd, // hi ɔ́lwɛz fáɪndz bráɪt aɪdɪəz tə səgdʒést.

9. hi névər sɪ́z ə búk, // ən tráɪz tə fərgɛ́t hɪz stédɪz. 10. hi fíəlz ðət vəkéʃənz ʃud bi sévrəl

yfərz lóŋ.

I. Read aloud several pages from a book you are studying, concentrating your attention on the correct pronunciation of final voiced consonants.

LESSON IX

L, R, and Syllabic Consonants

I. The Formation of [l] and [r].

Phoneticians sometimes classify [l] and [r] as glides. Other consonants are made with the speech organs in a more or less fixed position, but glides are characterized by the fact that they are formed as the organs of speech move from one place to another. Thus [w], another glide, is begun with the lips protruding and rounded, and is pronounced as the lips move from this position to the position required for whatever vowel sound may follow the [w].

Speakers of English normally pronounce [l] with the tip of the tongue touching the tooth ridge (just behind the upper teeth). *It is important to note that the sides of the tongue do not touch anything;* the middle of the tongue is low, and the air goes out over both sides. If [l] follows a vowel, as in *call* [kɔl], the tongue, lips, etc., move from the position of the vowel to the [l]-position. During this motion, the vocal cords vibrate continuously, since [l] is a voiced sound. It is the movement from one position to another which determines the characteristic sound of [l]. If the [l] precedes a vowel, as in *lie* [laɪ], the motion is from the [l]-position to the position of the vowel.

Pronounce *coal* [kɔl], *fool* [ful], *pull* [pʊl], *like* [laɪk], and *long* [lɔŋ], being certain that your speech organs take the proper positions.

[r] is a somewhat more complex sound. In certain parts of England, and the East and South of the United States, the letter hardly seems to be pronounced at all, except at the beginning of a word or syllable. A large majority of English-speaking people, however, pronounce it with both sides of the tongue touching the back part of the tooth ridge and the back teeth. *It is important to note that the tongue tip does not touch*

anything; the middle of the tongue, including the tip,
is lower than the sides, and the air goes out through
the channel formed between the middle of the tongue and
the roof of the mouth. The lips are slightly open. The
glide, the characteristic [r]-sound, is produced as the
speech organs move to this position from a vowel, as in
are [ɑr], or away from this position to a vowel, as in
red [rɛd]. In whatever direction the movement may end,
*it always begins by a motion toward the back of the
mouth.* More than any other factor, it is this retroflex
(toward the back) motion that gives the English [r] its
typical sound. The tongue tip rises a little and is
curved backward, while the sides of the tongue slide
along the back part of the tooth ridge as along two
rails.

Pronounce the vowel [ɑ]. As you do so, curve the
tip of your tongue up and slide the sides of the tongue
backward along the tooth ridge, and you should have no
difficulty in producing a perfect American [r].

When [r] follows a vowel, *or* [ɔr], the entire
movement is in a backward direction. When [r] precedes
a vowel, *right* [raɪt], the backward movement is very
brief, and is almost immediately reversed as the tongue
moves forward again to the vowel position.

Many speakers of German, French, and certain other
languages use a "uvular" r, made by vibrating the uvula
(the little flap of flesh which hangs down at the en-
trance of the throat) or by the friction produced as
the air passes between the uvula and the raised back
portion of the tongue. This type of r is also a glide,
characterized by movement of the speech organs, but to
produce it the tongue slides a little forward, rather
than backward, and the muscles of the soft palate are
tensed. Students who find it difficult to avoid this
type of r in English should concentrate on the *backward* movement of the tongue and making the uvula and
soft palate (the soft back part of the roof of the
mouth) remain motionless and relaxed.

The trilled r, typical of such languages as Spanish and Italian, can best be avoided by concentrating
on the sliding of the sides of the tongue along the
tooth ridge, by keeping the tongue tip comparatively
inactive, and by being very careful that the tip does
not approach closely the roof of the mouth or upper
teeth.

Japanese and Chinese students, in particular,
sometimes have difficulty in distinguishing between [l]
and [r]. They should spend a great deal of time pro-

nouncing such pairs of words as *grass* [græs] and *glass* [glæs], *crime* [kraɪm] and *climb* [klaɪm], *free* [fri] and *flee* [fli], *red* [rɛd] and *led* [lɛd], making the tip of the tongue touch the tooth ridge for [l] and stay away from the roof of the mouth and teeth for [r]. In a sense, [l] and [r] are made in exactly opposite ways: for [l] the tongue tip touches the tooth ridge and the air goes out over the sides; for [r] the sides of the tongue touch the tooth ridge while the air goes out over the middle and tip.

II. L and R after Front Vowels.

In Lesson II we learned to classify [i], [ɪ], [e], [ɛ], and [æ] as front vowels, [ɑ], [ɔ], [o], [ʊ], [u] and [ə] as back vowels. If the reasons for this classification and the meaning of the vowel triangle are not clear to you now, it might be well to review the lesson at this point.

Both [l] and [r] are produced rather far back in the mouth; they are nearer the back vowels than the front vowels. As a result, it is a more complicated process and takes more time to pass from a front vowel to [l] or [r] than from a back vowel to these consonants. Compare *ill* and *all*, *ear* and *or*. As the speech organs move back from the position of the front vowel, they pass through the middle, neutral zone where [ə] is formed. We may say then that:

WHEN A FRONT VOWEL IS FOLLOWED BY [l] OR [r], AN INTERMEDIARY [ə] IS INSERTED.

No such [ə] appears between a back vowel and [l] or [r], since the movement begins and ends in the back of the mouth without passing through the middle zone. We pronounce *wall* as [wɔl], but *well* as [wɛəl]. In the same way, among words in which [r] follows a vowel, we hear *car* [kɑr] without the intermediary sound, and *care* [kɛər] with it.

The deliberate insertion of [ə] in the cases just described will usually help a foreign student to produce an [l] and [r] which "sound American," and will enable him to avoid the "clear"[1] l which is a prominent fea-

---
1. Many phoneticians say that in English there are two kinds of l: a "clear" l, heard at the beginning of a word or syllable and after back vowels, made with the middle of the tongue held high; and a "dark" l, occurring after front vowels and produced as the middle of the tongue falls comparatively low in the mouth. These two l's, of course, correspond to our [l] and [əl]. The latter are preferred in this text for pedagogical reasons, and also to make it possible to call attention in written diagnoses to incorrect "clear" l's.

ture of many foreign accents in such words as *will*, *bell*, and *feel*. The latter should be pronounced [wɪəl], [bɛəl], and [fiəl], instead of [wɪl], [bɛl], and [fil].

The insertion of [ə] is usually not so easy to hear in words like *hilly* [hílɪ], in which the [l] is followed by another vowel sound, as it is in words such as *hill* [hɪəl], in which the [l] is final or followed by another consonant sound. The same is true for words with [r]: *merry* [mɛ́rɪ], without [ə]; but *where* [hwɛər], with [ə].

III. Syllabic Consonants.

English-speaking people are accustomed to thinking that every syllable must include at least one vowel, yet in words such as *little, sudden*, and *wouldn't* there are only consonant sounds in the final syllable. These are known as syllabic consonants, since they may make up a syllable without the accompaniment of vowels. In phonetic transcription syllabic consonants are indicated by drawing a short vertical line below them: *little* [lɪtl̩], *sudden* [sədn̩], *wouldn't* [wʊdn̩t]. They are difficult for most foreign students to pronounce; in place of [lɪtl̩] we frequently hear [lɪtəl] or [lɪl], in place of [wʊdn̩t] the student may say [wʊdənt] or [wʊnt], etc.

Syllabic consonants occur when a syllable ends in [t], [d], or [n], and the next syllable is <u>un</u>stressed and contains an [l] or [n]. This may be expressed by an equation:

$$\left.\begin{matrix}t\\d\\n\end{matrix}\right\} + \text{unstressed syllable containing} \left\{\begin{matrix}l\\n\end{matrix}\right. > \text{syllabic consonant.}$$

All the necessary conditions are present, for example, in *saddle* and *cotton*, and we have the pronunciations [sædl̩] and [katn̩]. In *lieutenant* [lutɛ́nənt], there is a [t] followed by an [n], but the [n] is in a stressed syllable, so no syllabic consonant results.

It is easy to remember the four consonants which are involved in syllabic consonants: [t], [d], [n], and [l]. They are the four which are formed with the tip of the tongue touching the tooth ridge.[2] Indeed, it is the fact

---

[2]. In rapid conversational speech, syllabic consonants may occur in two other cases where stops and continuants have the same points of articulation: 1) between [p] or [b] and [m], as in *stop 'em* [stapm̩]; and 2) between [k] or [g] and [ŋ], as in *I can go* [aɪkŋ̩go]. Since the alternate pronunciations, [stapəm] and [aɪkəngo], do not sound "foreign", these two cases are not important for the purposes of this text. Some phoneticians also transcribe as syllabic consonants such combinations as the [l] after the [s] in *pencil*, [pɛnsəl] or [pɛnsl̩], and the [l] after the [p] in *apple*, [æpəl] or [æpl̩], where the points of articulation are not quite identical. In these cases also, however, either alternate pronunciation is perfectly normal American.

that the four are all made with the tongue tip in the
same position that causes the formation of syllabic
consonants. What happens is that, in pronouncing *cotton*,
for example, the tongue tip goes to the tooth ridge to
form [ᵗ], *and just stays there to pronounce the following* [ⁿ]. There should not even be a brief separation of
tip and tooth ridge between [ᵗ] and [ⁿ]. If the tongue
tip breaks contact and moves from its fixed position
for even a fraction of a second, it will result in the
insertion of an [ə] between the two consonants. In a
word such as *cotton*, an [ə] in the second syllable is
definitely an element of "foreign accent."

You will remember that the formation of a stop,
like [t] or [d], usually requires two movements: a
closure, or stopping of the outflow of air, and then a
release of the air. Before a syllabic consonant, in
words like *little* and *sudden*, the closure for the stop
takes place normally, as the tongue tip makes contact
with the tooth ridge. But the release is quite unusual,
since the tongue tip, which normally makes the release
by moving away from the tooth ridge, must in this case
remain in its position for the formation of the following syllabic consonant. Before syllabic [ˡ] the release is made by a sudden lowering of the *sides* -- not
the *tip* -- of the tongue; this permits the air imprisoned by the preceding closure to rush out and make an
[ḷ]. Before syllabic [ⁿ] the release is made by a sudden opening of the velum, which allows the imprisoned
air to escape through the nose. (The velum is the soft
part of the palate, at the back of the roof of the
mouth. When drawn up, it closes the nasal passages, and
all escaping breath must come out through the mouth;
when relaxed and open, the breath may come out through
either nose or mouth.)

So, when you wish to pronounce a word like *little*
[lɪtḷ] or *sudden* [sədṇ], bring the tongue into contact
with the tooth ridge sharply and definitely for the [ᵗ]
or [ᵈ]. Then, *as you force the tongue tip to remain
where it is*, make the release which will produce [ˡ] or
[ⁿ]. You may find it helpful at the beginning to pronounce the first syllable completely, [lɪt], and to
pause on the [ᵗ] in order to feel and maintain the
pressure of the tongue tip in its proper position before you go on to make the release and pronounce the
last syllable, [ḷ]. In the same way, try *important*:
[ɪmpɔ́rt], pause,[ṇt]; and *sentence*, [sɛnt], pause, [ṇs].

It should be noted that the [t] which precedes a
syllabic [ˡ], as in *little*, is the "[d]-like [t]" discussed at the end of Section I, Lesson VIII.

IV. Exercises.

A. This drill is intended to furnish you with an opportunity for extensive and careful practice in the correct formation of [r]. It begins with the combinations in which most students usually find it easiest to make an American [r], and then moves on to more difficult combinations. Pronounce each item three or four times, more if necessary, keeping in mind the instructions given in Section I. Try to master each step in the exercise before you go on to the next one.

1. a. ɑr b. ər c. ɔr d. ɛər e. ɪər
2. a. kɑr b. fɔr c. sər d. hɪər e. ðɛər
3. a. fɑrm b. bərn c. gərl d. mɛðər e. fɑðər
4. a. mɔ́rnɪŋ b. bɑ́rgɪn c. wɜ́rkɪŋ d. wɔ́rmər e. bɔ́rdər
5. a. ɑrɑ b. ɑro c. ɑri d. ərə e. ərɛ
6. a. mɛ́rɪ b. kɛ́rɪ c. mɑ́rəl d. fyúrɪ e. ərɑ́und
7. a. ri b. re c. rɑ d. rɔ e. ru
8. a. rɪd b. ren c. rɛk d. ræpɪŋ e. rɪfər
9. a. rəf b. rol c. rɑɪd d. rɑuz e. rúlər
10. a. tri b. pre c. dro d. fro e. gru
11. a. θrɪŋ b. krɛt c. θrɑn d. grɑundrɪd e. prɪpɛ́ər
12. a. ɛvrɪ b. əpréz c. ɔɪfrɛ́nd d. dɪkrɑ́ɪ e. bɪgrɛ́dz

13. a. a large farm. b. shorter working hours. c. to further your purposes. d. for ever and ever. e. the wrong room. f. a greater artist. g. frequent arrivals. h. to cross the border. i. a brown dress. j. to bring under control.

B. Your instructor will pronounce the following names of cities with an "American accent." Imitate him as closely as possible, paying special attention to the formation of [r]:

1. Bergen
2. Berlin
3. Bern
4. Cairo
5. Dairen [dɑɪrɛ́n]
6. Ferrara
7. Florida
8. France
9. Hiroshima
10. Madrid
11. Nuremberg
12. Paris
13. Peru
14. Prague
15. Rio de Janeiro
16. Rumania
17. Smyrna
18. Tripoli
19. Teherαn [tɪərɑ́n]
20. Warsaw

C. This exercise is for Oriental students. Pronounce each pair of words several times, remembering the differences between [l] and [r] as described in the last paragraph of Section I. In each case the two words sound exactly alike, except for [l] and [r].

1. shall, share
2. alive, arrive
3. believe, bereave
4. late, rate

American English Pronunciation 95

5. liver, river
6. blight, bright
7. cloud, crowd
8. play, pray
9. blush, brush
10. glue, grew
11. glass, grass
12. fly, fry

D. In the light of what you learned in Section II of this lesson, determine which of the following words would be pronounced with an [ə] inserted between the vowel sound and [l] or [r]. Then transcribe all the words in phonetic symbols, and check them with your instructor's transcription. Finally, pronounce your transcriptions, taking particular care to avoid "clear" l's where they should not be heard.

1. bar
2. for
3. hair
4. ear
5. care
6. beer
7. bear
8. they're
9. we're
10. fur
11. sir
12. word
13. heard
14. verb
15. will
16. tell
17. coal
18. kill
19. real
20. all
21. full
22. ill
23. fell
24. ball
25. shall
26. doll
27. pool
28. spelled
29. failed
30. she'll

E. Three of the words in the following exercise do not contain syllabic consonants, but all the others do. Which are the three exceptions? Draw a line under the syllabic consonants in the other twenty-nine words (see Section III); then pronounce the entire exercise. Your instructor should pronounce this material with you, before you try to work on it alone.

1. little
2. didn't
3. student
4. couldn't
5. article
6. tunnel
7. Latin
8. harden
9. idle
10. important
11. mountain
12. hospital
13. travel
14. curtain
15. oriental
16. bottle
17. saddled
18. broadened
19. attention
20. battleship
21. suddenly
22. sentences
23. gardening
24. certainty
25. penalty
26. finally
27. fertilize

28. ordinary
29. ventilate
30. monotonous
31. bread and butter
32. bright and early

F. Practice the following exercise several times, concentrating your attention on a different feature at each reading: 1) intonation, 2) the correct formation of [r], 3) inserting an [ə] between front vowels and [l], 4) syllabic consonants. In a final reading, try to combine the four features satisfactorily.

1. Bill likes nothing so well as mountain

climbing. 2. He will tell you how important it is to start early. 3. If he doesn't feel like walking, he ordinarily rides a brown horse. 4. The trail is easier when dry weather has hardened the ground. 5. As he climbs, he rests very little until he has reached the top. 6. The clouds hang like a curtain over the river below him. 7. The horse looks in the brush for green grass. 8. Bill likes to leave the trail and ride right down the mountainside. 9. Once he fell and hurt his ankle; he still limps a little. 10. But Bill didn't tell anyone a word about it when he finally arrived back home. 11. Some day, he'll kill himself or end up in the hospital. 12. I wouldn't care for anything so strenuous and risky myself. 13. I prefer gardening, but

Bill finds it a little monotonous. 14. I cer-

tainly couldn't get up so bright and early in

the morning. 15. I must be paying the penalty

of idleness; that's the real reason.

G. 1. As you answer these questions, use the intonation which is normal for a series (see
Lesson VI, end of Section II):

   a. What do you usually eat for breakfast?
   b. What languages do you speak?
   c. What courses are you taking now?
   d. What countries have you visited?
   e. What kinds of ice cream have you tried
      in this country?

2. Make questions in which you present the following ideas as alternatives with *or*: for
example, "Is the food better in *the United
States*, or in *your native country*?" Be careful with the intonation of the questions
(see Lesson VI, end of Section II).

   a. interesting, boring?
   b. a real fire, a false alarm?
   c. just beginning, ending?
   d. this school, the school you last attended?
   e. Monday, Tuesday, Wednesday?

H. This lesson ends with a speed and rhythm drill.
Read it at normal conversational speed, and try
to observe an even, regular sentence rhythm
(see Lesson IV, Section I). The material is
well suited for individual laboratory work with
a sound mirror or tape recorder.

  1. a. I found it.
     b. I've told you I found it.
     c. I've told you already that I found it.
     d. I've told you already that I found it at
        the movies.
     e. I've told you already that I found the
        money at the movies.
     f. I've told you already that I found the
        money at the movies on Sunday.

2. a. I'm surprised!
   b. I'm surprised you believe it!
   c. I'm surprised you believed such a story!
   d. I'm surprised you believed such an incredible story!
   e. I'm surprised that anyone believed such an incredible story!
   f. I'm surprised that anyone believed such an incredible story as that!
3. a. He knows everything.
   b. He appears to know everything.
   c. He sometimes appears to know everything.
   d. He sometimes appears to know everything when he lectures.
   e. He sometimes appears to know everything when he lectures so confidently.
   f. He sometimes appears to know everything when he lectures so confidently to his classes.

I. Outside of class, read aloud several pages of simple, conversational material, concentrating your attention on the pronunciation of [l], or [r], whichever seems to give you most trouble.

LESSON X

Front Vowels

I. Vowel Substitutions.

A common - and very serious - mistake made by students of English is the substitution of one vowel for another in the stressed syllable of a word: for example, the pronunciation of *leaving* as [lɪvɪŋ] instead of [livɪŋ]. Such a substitution is serious because it often changes completely the meaning of the word. It may be a very good thing to tell your friend, "[aɪ hop yu wont liv naʊ]"; but "[aɪ hop yu wont lɪv naʊ]" may lead to a misunderstanding.

The usual causes for mistakes of this sort seem to be:

1. The speaker gives the letters which represent vowels the sounds they would have in his native language. A Frenchman tends to pronounce *aid* as [ɛd], instead of [ed].

2. The speaker is deceived by the inconsistencies of English spelling. Usually *ar* is pronounced [ar], as in *car*, *far*, and *part*; therefore *war* is sometimes wrongly pronounced as [war] instead of [wɔr].

3. The speaker cannot hear, and consequently cannot reproduce, the difference between two sounds, either because the two do not exist in his original language, or because they never serve to distinguish between words in it. Both [e] and [ɛ] are heard in Spanish, but there are no two Spanish words which are exactly alike, except that one contains [e] and the other [ɛ]. As a result, the student from Mexico often mispronounces *change* as [tʃɛndʒ].

Lessons X, XI, XII, and XIII attack the problem of stressed vowel substitutions. They are intended to give you practice in hearing and reproducing the differences

between vowels which are frequently confused, to give
you an opportunity to make stronger associations between vowel sounds and their usual spelling, and call
your attention to certain common words in which the
vowel sounds are spelled in an unusual way.

II. The Vowel [i].

The material which follows is based on the vowel
triangle, as explained in Lesson II. It would be well
at this point to review that explanation if you do not
have it well in mind.

You may remember that [i] is the vowel which is
pronounced farthest to the front of the mouth, with
the jaw most nearly closed. *The sides of the tongue are
pressed tightly against the upper bicuspid (two-pointed)
teeth and the palate (roof of the mouth).* The tongue
tip may *press the cutting edge of the lower front teeth.
Upper and lower teeth almost touch. The lips are spread
somewhat by muscular force. The air escapes through a
very narrow opening between the tongue blade (the part
just behind the tip) and the upper tooth ridge.* In
general, [i] is made with a great deal of tension and
effort. You may be able to pronounce it better if you
think of it as being written with a double symbol:
[ii].

This is the vowel heard in *she* [ʃi], *seem* [sim],
leave [liv], *chief* [tʃif], etc. Say these words carefully; then pronounce the vowel in each of them alone:
[ʃi], [ʃi], [ʃi], [i], [i], [i]. As you pronounce, see
that your tongue, teeth, and lips take the position described in the preceding paragraph.

III. [ɪ].

The vowel which follows [i], as we move away from
the front of the mouth, is [ɪ]. To change [i] to [ɪ],
*the jaw relaxes and drops very slightly, the pressure
of the sides of the tongue against the upper bicuspids
decreases, and the forced spreading of the lips dis-
appears. The tongue tip may merely touch the back of
the lower front teeth.* To see clearly what happens to
lips, jaw, and tongue, it is best to watch your mouth
in a hand mirror as you form [i] and [ɪ]. *Most important of all, the opening between the tongue blade and
the palate becomes wider and rounder.* This means that
the place where tongue and palate are closest together
moves a little farther back in the mouth.

Pronounce *sheep* [ʃip], then *ship* [ʃɪp]. Now just
the vowels of the two words: [i], [ɪ], [i], [ɪ], [i], [ɪ].

etc. Can you feel the essential differences in the position of the speech organs clearly? Form an [i]-sound; then, without interrupting the flow of breath, try to make the [i] change to an [ɪ] by appropriate movements of the tongue, jaw, and lips.

[ɪ] is the vowel of *big* [bɪg], *king* [kɪŋ], and *city* [sɪtɪ]. In some languages it does not exist. In others it may be heard occasionally, but does not differentiate words from similar words containing [i]. Students who learned these other languages first will probably have difficulty in distinguishing clearly between *leave* [liv] and *live* [lɪv]. Very often they will use, instead of [i] or [ɪ], a vowel half way between the two, which will make *leave* sound like *live*, or *live* like *leave*, to an American ear.

[i]-for-[ɪ] or [ɪ]-for-[i] is, in fact, by far the most common and troublesome of the vowel substitutions we spoke of at the beginning of this lesson.

IV. [e].

Moving on downward and backward on the vowel triangle, from [ɪ] we come to [e]. *The jaw drops just a little more. The tongue tip may touch the bottom of the front teeth without pressure. The sides of the tongue press slightly against the sides of the upper bicuspids. The passage through which the air escapes between the middle of the tongue and the palate grows wider. The lips are open and relaxed.*

Perhaps the characteristic which best distinguishes [e] is that *it is usually pronounced as a slight diphthong,* beginning as [e] and ending as [ɪ]. Some phoneticians write this vowel as [eɪ] or [e¹]. The complete vowel begins in the [e]-position described in the preceding paragraph, then moves upward and forward to the [ɪ]-position as the tongue is pushed nearer the palate and upper front teeth.

The degree of diphthongization is greatest in a word pronounced with an inflection at the end of an intonation pattern:

It's the hand of fate [ɪts ðə hænd əv feɪt] (see

Lesson V, Section II); in a word where the [e] is followed by a final voiced consonant: *made* [meɪd], *rave* [reɪv] (see Lesson VIII, Section II); or in a word where the [e] is final: *day* [deɪ].

The diphthongization is also much greater in most varieties of British English than in American English. In this text the [eɪ]-symbol is not normally used, since its use might encourage the student to make exaggerated diphthongs which would be too noticeable and would not sound American.

[e] is the vowel heard in *say* [se], *plain* [plen], and *came* [kem]. It is most often confused with [ɛ] and [æ]. Can you see the difference between [e], [ɪ], and [i] in your mirror?

V. [ɛ].

After [e] on the triangle comes [ɛ]; but, unlike [e], [ɛ] is not usually diphthongized. *To form* [ɛ], *the jaw is once more lowered just a little. For the first time, the tongue exerts no pressure at all.* The tongue tip may touch the spot where the lower front teeth join the tooth ridge, *the sides touch lightly the tips of the upper bicuspids. The air-escape passage is as wide as the roof of the mouth itself.*

[ɛ] is the vowel of *yes* [yɛs], *egg* [ɛg] and *end* [ɛnd]. It is not so clear a sound as [e], from which it must be carefully distinguished. Make sure you have understood and seen the chief differences: [ɛ] is not diphthongized, and in forming it the sides of the tongue touch lightly the tips of the upper bicuspids without pressure. For [e] there is enough pressure to narrow the air-passage somewhat.

VI. [æ].

The last of the front vowels is [æ]. *To form it the jaw is lowered quite a bit, until the mouth is almost as wide open as it can be without making a muscular effort.* Remember that this is the last front vowel that can be made; when we move on to [ɑ], the sides and tip of the tongue will no longer touch the upper or lower teeth at all. *For* [æ], *the lightest possible contact is made between tongue tip and lower tooth ridge, and between sides of tongue and the tips of the upper bicuspids or even of the first molar teeth just behind the bicuspids. In* other words, *the passage through which the air escapes is as wide and deep as it can be and still remain a passage formed by the tongue rather than by the cheeks.*

[æ] is the vowel of *am* [æm], *black* [blæk], and *cap* [kæp]. It is easily confused with [ɑ], [ɛ], or even [e]. Before you go on to the next section of this lesson, it would be well to go over the entire series -- [i-ɪ-e-ɛ-æ]--many times with your mirror, checking your way of forming the sounds with the physiological descriptions of how they should be formed.

VII. Exercises.

A. 1. Listen carefully to your instructor as he pronounces a prolonged [i] several times: i-i-i, i-i-i, i-i-i. Imitate his pronunciation of the vowel, watching your lips, tongue, teeth, etc., in a hand mirror, and trying to make your speech organs assume the exact position described in the appropriate section of this lesson.

2. Listen, then imitate, as your instructor pronounces the following material. Finally, try to pronounce each word or phrase to his satisfaction. If he finds that the vowel in any word does not sound quite right, correct yourself by making your speech organs assume more exactly the desired position:

a. bi
b. mi
c. fri
d. itʃ
e. ist
f. ʃip
g. sik
h. nid
i. fit
j. kwin

k. these dreams
l. weak tea
m. please teach me
n. the green trees
o. to meet in the street
p. rid, rɪd
q. hit, hɪt
r. slip, slɪp
s. mit, mɛt
t. fid, fɛd

B. (The instructions for Exercise A apply also to Exercises B, C, D, and E.)

1. ɪ-ɪ-ɪ, ɪ-ɪ-ɪ, ɪ-ɪ-ɪ

2. a. bɪt
b. fɪks
c. kɪs
d. rɪŋ
e. trɪp
f. wɪn
g. lɪft
h. ɪts
i. ɪf
j. ɪŋk

k. this city
l. which gift
m. six inches
n. a quick finish
o. to visit my sister
p. sɪt, sit
q. lɪp, lip
r. stɪk, stek
s. mɪs, mɛs
t. sɪns, sɛns

C. 1. e-e-e, e-e-e, e-e-e

2. a. pe   k. straight pay
   b. se   l. a date at eight
   c. gre   m. a famous flavor
   d. et   n. the baby's name
   e. edʒ   o. he made me late
   f. ren   p. plen, plæn
   g. led   q. gres, græs
   h. wet   r. get, gɛt
   i. pent   s. bled, blɛd
   j. plez   t. tek, tɪk

D. 1. ɛ-ɛ-ɛ, ɛ-ɛ-ɛ, ɛ-ɛ-ɛ
   2. a. stɛp   k. send them
      b. tɛn   l. a red head
      c. lɛg   m. several presents
      d. prɛs   n. her best dress
      e. nɛkst   o. when I left
      f. lɛŋθ   p. bɛd, bæd
      g. frɛʃ   q. mɛn, mæn
      h. ɛg   r. lɛt, let
      i. ɛnd   s. rɛst, rest
      j. ɛdʒ   t. wɛəl, wɪəl

E. 1. æ-æ-æ, æ-æ-æ, æ-æ-æ
   2. a. bæk   k. narrow path
      b. bæŋk   l. past master
      c. fæst   m. half a glass
      d. glæd   n. a happy fancy
      e. pæs   o. a grand family
      f. plænt   p. bænd, bɛnd
      g. ræg   q. læst, lɛst
      h. æz   r. sæd, sɛd
      i. æsk   s. æd, ed
      j. ækt   t. hæt, hat

F. It is suggested that five steps be carried out
   in doing each of the two parts of the following
   drill: 1) be sure that the students understand the meaning of all the words; 2) let the
   teacher read across the columns and the students imitate him; 3) have the students read
   collectively and individually across the columns; 4) let the teacher dictate ten words selected at random from the drill, and the students write down the words they hear; 5) the
   students pick out certain words and try to
   pronounce them so well that the teacher can
   recognize them.

   1.   i   ɪ   ɛ
       a. peak   g. pick   m. peck

American English Pronunciation

	b. dean	h. din	n. den
	c. deed	i. did	o. dead
	d. least	j. list	p. lest
	e. heed	k. hid	q. head
	f. feel	l. fill	r. fell

2.   e   ɛ   æ

	a. bait	g. bet	m. bat
	b. pain	h. pen	n. pan
	c. bake	i. beck	o. back
	d. laid	j. led	p. lad
	e. lace	k. less	q. lass
	f. shale	l. shell	r. shall

G. Most of the following sound combinations do not make up English words. First, pronounce them in imitation of your instructor. Then, he will dictate twenty or more combinations chosen from the list at random, while you try to copy down in symbols the sounds he makes.

1. ʃi   7. ʃɪ   13. ʃe   19. ʃɛ   25. ʃæ
2. ʃip   8. ʃɪp   14. ʃep   20. ʃɛp   26. ʃæp
3. rim   9. rɪm   15. rem   21. rɛm   27. ræm
4. liv   10. lɪv   16. lev   22. lɛv   28. læv
5. fit   11. fɪt   17. fet   23. fɛt   29. fæt
6. sig   12. sɪg   18. seg   24. sɛg   30. sæg

H. Read each of the sentences below twice, using word <u>a</u> in the first reading and word <u>b</u> in the second. Then read again and use either <u>a</u> or <u>b</u>, while another member of the class tries to identify in each case the word that you pronounced.

1. (a. wean) (b. win) It's time to _____ the child.
2. (a. feel)(b. fill) He doesn't seem to _____ the need.
3. (a. peak)(b. pick) He walked confidently toward the _____.
4. (a. dean)(b. din) I can't study because of the _____.
5. (a. heed)(b. hid) We always _____ our mistakes.
6. (a. sheep)(b. ship) You can't get a _____ into such a small place.
7. (a. bit)(b. bet) I'd like to make a little _____ on that horse.
8. (a. pin)(b. pen) Keep the _____ where you can reach it.
9. (a. pig)(b. peg) I caught the _____ with both hands.

10. (a. rain)(b. wren) The _____ descends gently from the clouds.
11. (a. dale)(b. dell) A great many flowers grow in the _____.
12. (a. laid)(b. led) Who could have _____ the child there?
13. (a. date)(b. debt) I'll never forget that old _____ of mine.
14. (a. mate)(b. mat) The dog was asleep by his _____.
15. (a. cane)(b. can) The cook has a _____ in her hand.
16. (a. mess)(b. mass) In the street was a tangled _____ of cars.
17. (a. pet)(b. pat) It's not wise to _____ a tiger.
18. (a. ten)(b. tan) She's very proud of her _____ shoes.
19. (a. peck)(b. pack) You'll need a whole _____ of cards.
20. (a. shell)(b. shall) You'll shell more peas than I _____.

If the instructor so wishes, the above drill may be used as a test of your ability to distinguish between the front vowel sounds. Take a piece of paper and number the lines from 1 through 20. The instructor will read each sentence, inserting one of the two test words. You should decide which one he used and write <u>a</u> or <u>b</u> on your paper opposite the number of the sentence.

I. Read these sentences aloud, making as clear a distinction as possible between the vowels of the words in italics:

1. Either *read* the book or get *rid* of it.
2. Didn't you buy *it* to *eat*?
3. I didn't *seek* to be *sick*.
4. *Each* foot *itches*.
5. *List* at *least* the most important ones.
6. She *dipped deeply* into the sack.
7. Don't *grin* at my *greenness*.
8. They *begged* a *big* meal.
9. There was a sharp noise as the ball *met* his *mitt*.
10. The living influenced us more than the *dead did*.
11. Can you *lift* what's *left*?
12. You'll get *wet* if you *wait*.
13. *Tell* us a *tale*, grandma.

14. There's a *gate* to *get* through.
15. I hope long *dresses* are a *fading fad*.
16. Bankers *lend* money on *land*.
17. He *said* he was *sad*.
18. His bad *leg* made him *lag* behind.
19. The hen *sat* where he *set* her.
20. You've certainly *met* your *match*.

J. Read these sentences with two different intonation patterns: 1) so as to create suspense between the two parts of the sentence, and 2) without suspense (see Lesson VI, Section II).

1. If you do that again, I'll punish you.
2. You push a little button, and the food comes out.
3. I opened the door, and there was the "ghost".
4. When he heard the answer, he was horrified.
5. If it happens here, it will be the ruin of us.
6. Until you see me, make no move.
7. If I'd known that, I could have made ten dollars.
8. Smoke one of these, and you'll never smoke again.

K. The intonation patterns marked in the selection which follows are somewhat more varied and freer than most of those you have worked with before. Can you control your voice as the line indicates? This is a good passage for recording.

1. "nō, ðɪs bŭk ɪz nɑ́t ɪgzǽktlɪ frī́. // ən yét ɪt ɪz frī́ // ɪn ðə séns ðət yu wónt ǽkt∫uəlɪ bi péɪŋ for ɪt. 2. hwɑt yu wīəl bi péɪŋ for // ɪz ə θrī́-yīər səbskrɪ́p∫ən tə gúd hōmz mǽgəzīn. 3. ən yul bi péɪŋ ðɪ ɪgzǽkt prɑ́ɪs yud pé ɪf yu wént tə yur lókəl dīələr. 4. bət baɪ tékɪŋ ə səbskrɪ́p∫ən

naυ from mĭ. // yu ɔ́lso wɪəl rɪsív ðɪs bʊ́k əv
fáɪv héndrəd tĕstɪd résɪpiz. 5. só, yu sĭ. // ɪn
ə mǽnər əv spíkɪŋ. // ðɪs bʊ́k ɪz ǽbsəlútlɪ frí.
6. ən hwíts mór. // mǽdəm. // yur pərmítɪd tə tĕk,
ɪt naυ, lʊk ɪt óvər, ən rɪtə́rn ɪt tə mí //ɪf yu,
dɪsáɪd yu dont kér tə tĕk ə səbskrípʃən tə gʊ́d
hómz mægəzĭn." 7. hi smáɪld trɑɪə́mfəntlɪ ət
hər. 8. kʊd énɪθɪŋ bi fárər ðæn ðǽt?

(Adapted from the story "Profession: House-
wife." by Sally Benson, originally published
in The New Yorker .)

L. Read aloud several pages of English, concentrating your attention on the correct formation of the front vowel with which you seem to
   have most difficulty.

LESSON XI

Back Vowels

I. The Vowel [ɑ].

You have no doubt noticed that when you visit a physician, and he wishes to have a clear view into your mouth and throat, he asks you to say, "Ah." That is, of course, the sound of our vowel [ɑ]. The physician knows that the formation of [ɑ] requires the mouth to be opened more widely than does that of any other sound. The tongue is also lower in the mouth than for any other vowel. That is what gives him his unobstructed view.

More precisely, in order to form [ɑ], the jaw is lowered more than it would be in a normal relaxed position, lowered so far as to require a slight muscular effort. As a consequence, the lips are also wide open, about an inch apart for most speakers, and two upper front teeth and several lower teeth are probably visible. Verify this with your mirror. The tongue tip lightly touches a point as low on the floor of the mouth as it can reach, so low that in compensation the back of the tongue must be raised just a little in the throat.

[ɑ], in general American English, is the vowel of *father* [fɑðər], *box* [bɑks], and *calm* [kɑm]. It is most often confused with [ə] and [æ]. What are the essential differences in the formation of [æ] and [ɑ]? Check your answer with the description of [æ] in Lesson X and with your mirror.

II. [ɔ].

In moving from [ɑ] to [ɔ], we are starting up the back half of the vowel triangle. The most important thing to watch is the position of your lips. The value of a front vowel — [i], [ɪ], [e], [ɛ], or [æ] — is largely determined by the tongue; that is, by the shape and size of the air-escape passage between the tongue and the roof of the mouth. On the other hand, it is the lips — the size and shape of the opening between them — that have most influence in forming a back vowel. For [ɑ] this opening was about 1½ inches across, 1 inch from top to bottom, and shaped like this:

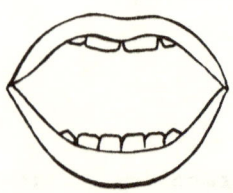

Lip Position for [ɑ]

For [ɔ] the opening is usually about 1 inch or less across, and ½ inch from top to bottom. The lips are somewhat protruded (pushed forward). Normally little is to be seen of the teeth.

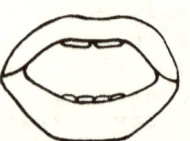

Lip Position for [ɔ]

In order for the lips to assume this position for [ɔ], the jaw is raised a little. The tongue remains in approximately the same position as for [ɑ], but is "bunched" a little more toward the back of the mouth.

[ɔ] is the vowel of *all* [ɔl], *saw* [sɔ], *cause* [kɔz], and *cross* [krɔs]. It is easily confused with [o] and [ə].

III. [o].

In order to produce an [o], the lips form the shape of the letter o. This requires that they be protruded and rounded more than for [ɔ]. The resulting opening is a little circle about ½ inch in diameter.

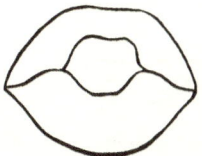

Lip Position for [o]

The jaw has been raised still more, and the "bunching" of the tongue in the back of the mouth is greater. The tongue tip probably no longer touches the floor of the mouth.

Like [e], [o] is frequently diphthongized, much more so in British than in American English (see Lesson X, Section IV). The complete vowel begins as a pure [o], made as pictured above, and moves on to a brief [ʊ] (see the picture of lip position for [ʊ] in Section IV). This means that during the pronunciation of the sound the lips may close slightly and lose their forced rounding. Some phoneticians write the diphthongized vowel as [oʊ] or [oᵁ].

[o] is the vowel found in *go* [go], *cold* [kold], *coast* [kost], *door* [dor], *soul* [sol], and *blow* [blo]. It is sometimes confused with [ɔ] and [u]. What are the essential differences between [o] and [ɔ]? Can you see them with your hand mirror?

IV. [ʊ].

Up to now, in order to make the classification of vowels as simple as possible, we have assumed that the progression from [o] through [ʊ] to [u] was perfectly regular: that as we moved from one vowel to another up the back half of the triangle we merely raised the jaw, rounded the lips, and pulled the tongue backward a little more each time. Actually, the relationship between the back vowels is more complex than that; the regular progression will account for [ɔ], [o], and [u], but not altogether for [ʊ].

To form [ʊ] the lips are, in fact, *less* rounded and protruded than in the production of [o], the preceding vowel. The opening between them is wider across than for [o], but a good bit smaller in distance from upper to lower lip. As in the case of [ɑ], in the formation of [ʊ] the teeth are clearly visible; the tips of the lower teeth approach the backs of the upper ones quite closely.

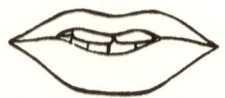

Lip Position for [ʊ]

Though the tongue tip touches nothing, the tongue itself is pulled back and up, more than for [o], until its sides touch the upper tooth ridge.

[ʊ] is the vowel of *book* [bʊk], *full* [fʊl], and *could* [kʊd]. It is most often confused with [u] and [ə].

V. [u].

Like [i] at the other extreme of the triangle, [u] requires tension and effort for its production. It may help you to make the necessary effort if you think of the sound as being written with a double symbol: [uu]. The lips should be rounded and protruded as much as possible, leaving a little circular opening about the size of a pencil. The teeth are not visible.

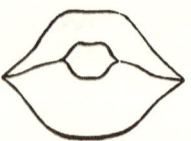

Lip Position for [u]

The tip of the tongue is drawn quite far back and touches nothing, but the sides of the tongue press firmly for some distance along the upper tooth ridge.

[u] is the vowel of *too* [tu], and *blue* [blu]. It is easily confused with [ʊ]. Form the two sounds carefully before your hand mirror until you can see and feel clearly the essential difference: 1) in the rounding and protrusion of the lips; 2) in the pressure exerted by the tongue; 3) in the position of the teeth.

This would be an excellent place, in fact, to go through the entire series — [ɑ-o-ɔ-ʊ-u] — before your mirror, trying to fix in your mind the distinguishing characteristics of the formation of each vowel.

VI. [ə].

The only remaining vowel sound is the central, neutral, relaxed, "lazy" [ə], which is not properly a part of either the front or back series. It has already been described at some length in Lessons II and III, in connection with its very frequent use in unstressed syllables. However, it may be well here to add a few more details, by way of comparison, now that you have a clearer understanding of the physiology of the other vowel sounds.

[ə] *is formed with the lips slightly parted over almost their entire length:*

Lip Position for [ə]

There is no tension or effort anywhere. The tongue lies relaxed on the floor of the mouth, and usually neither its sides nor its tip touches anything.

It is the vowel of *cut* [kət], *bird* [bərd], and *dull* [dəl]. Due to its central position, it may be confused with any of the other vowels, though this seems to happen most often with those in the back series, especially [ɑ], [ɔ], and [ʊ]. To change an [ə] into an [ɑ], all that is needed is to open the mouth too wide. To change [ə] to [ʊ], narrow the lip opening by putting some pressure on the corners of the mouth, touch the sides of the tongue against the upper tooth ridge, and move the teeth closer together.

Before [r], [ə] has a slightly different sound or "coloring", which results from the movements made by the speech organs as they prepare to form the [r]: *word* [wərd], *verb* [vərb].

VII. Exercises.

A. 1. Listen carefully to your instructor as he pronounces a prolonged [ɑ] several times: ɑ-ɑ-ɑ, ɑ-ɑ-ɑ, ɑ-ɑ-ɑ. Imitate his pronunciation of the vowel, watching your lips, teeth, etc., in a hand mirror, and trying to make your speech organs assume the exact position described in the appropriate section of this lesson.

2. Listen, then imitate, as your instructor pronounces the following material. Finally, try to pronounce each word or phrase to his satisfaction. If he finds that the vowel in a word does not sound quite right, correct yourself by making your speech organs assume more exactly the desired position:

a. ɑd
b. ɑks
c. ɑrm
d. drɑp
e. gɑd
f. klɑk
g. lɑt
h. mɑrtʃ
i. gɑrd
j. dɑrk
k. to start watching
l. from top to bottom
m. a garden party
n. a hot-rod car
o. to stock the shop
p. hat, hɑt
q. stak, stɑk
r. kap, kɑp
s. nat, nɑt
t. rak, ræk

B. (The instructions for Exercise A apply also to Exercises B, C, D, E, and F.)

1. ɔ-ɔ-ɔ, ɔ-ɔ-ɔ, ɔ-ɔ-ɔ
2. a. sɔ
b. pɔ
c. drɔ
d. ɔl
e. ɔf
f. krɔs
g. lɔŋ
h. sɔlt
i. kɔld
j. bɔrn
k. tall corn
l. small talk
m. across the walk
n. the horse's stall
o. a soft cloth
p. lɔ, lo
q. bɔl, bol
r. kɔst, kost
s. strɔŋ, strəŋ
t. wɔrd, wərd

C. 1. o-o-o, o-o-o, o-o-o
2. a. no
b. ðo
c. θro
d. old
e. od
f. bon
g. smok
h. post
i. not
j. hops
k. both soldiers
l. an open door
m. those snows
n. the fourth hole
o. his own show
p. flo, flɔ
q. kot, kɔt
r. noz, nɔz
s. kol, kul
t. roz, ruz

D. 1. ʊ-ʊ-ʊ, ʊ-ʊ-ʊ, ʊ-ʊ-ʊ
2. a. fʊt
b. pʊl
c. tʊk

American English Pronunciation 115

    d. hʊd   j. wʊlf   p. fʊl, ful
    e. nʊk   k. a good book   q. ʃʊd, ʃud
    f. yʊr   l. she could cook   r. wʊd, wud
    g. pʊʃ   m. put in sugar   s. pʊt, pət
    h. bʊʃ   n. stood by the brook   t. tʊk, tək
    i. wʊl   o. looking at the woman

E. 1. u-u-u, u-u-u, u-u-u
   2. a. tru   h. pruv   o. move into
       b. hu   i. tuθ   the room
       c. glu   j. gus   p. ʃut, ʃət
       d. fud   k. a loose tooth   q. sun, sən
       e. spul   l. through the school   r. luk luk
       f. frut   m. whose shoe   s. spuk, spok
       g. luz   n. a blue moon   t. tʃuz, tʃoz

F. 1. ə-ə-ə, ə-ə-ə, ə-ə-ə
   2. a. əp   h. wəns   o. wonderful
       b. əs   i. hər   company
       c. ərn   j. wərd   p. ʃət, ʃat
       d. ləŋ   k. mother tongue   q. klək, klak
       e. hənt   l. girl trouble   r. kəm, kam
       f. kəp   m. young love   s. kət, kɔt
       g. dəst   n. the ugly duckling   t. nən, nun

G. Did you ever try to read lips as the deaf must learn to do in order to understand what is said to them? The back vowels and certain consonants are rather easy to recognize by sight. Before doing the following exercise, it would be well to review the pictures of the lip position for back vowels and reread, if necessary, the material in Lesson VII on the point of articulation of [f] and [p]. Watch in your hand mirror as you form the sounds. In class your instructor will form some of the combinations below with his lips, tongue, etc. without actually uttering any sound. Try to recognize each combination and write down its number.

    1. a   4. ɔ   7. o   10. ʊ   13. u   16. ə
    2. fa   5. fɔ   8. fo   11. fʊ   14. fu   17. fə
    3. pa   6. pɔ   9. po   12. pʊ   15. pu   18. pə

H. The drills below are to be carried out like Exercise F of the preceding lesson: 1) the teacher makes sure that the meaning of all words is understood; 2) he reads across the column and the class imitates his pronunciation; 3) the students read across the columns as a group and individually; 4) the teacher dictates ten or more words selected at random; 5) the students pick out certain words and try to pronounce them so well that the teɑcher can identify them by letter.

1. ɑ   ə   ɔ
   - a. not
   - b. cod
   - c. Don
   - d. cot
   - e. ɑre
   - f. bɑrn
   - g. nut
   - h. cud
   - i. done
   - j. cut
   - k. err
   - l. burn
   - m. nɑught
   - n. cɑwed
   - o. dɑwn
   - p. cɑught
   - q. or
   - r. born

2. ɔ   o   u
   - a. flaw
   - b. Shaw
   - c. bought
   - d. call
   - e. Paul
   - f. lawn
   - g. flow
   - h. show
   - i. boat
   - j. coal
   - k. pole
   - l. loan
   - m. flew
   - n. shoe
   - o. boot
   - p. cool
   - q. pool
   - r. loon

3. ə   ʊ   u
   - a. luck
   - b. cud
   - c. buck
   - d. ____
   - e. putt
   - f. ____
   - g. look
   - h. could
   - i. book
   - j. should
   - k. put
   - l. pull
   - m. Luke
   - n. cooed
   - o. ____
   - p. shoed
   - q. ____
   - r. pool

I. Read each of the sentences below twice, using word **a** in the first reading and word **b** in the second. Then read again and use either **a** or **b**, while another member of the class tries to identify in each case the word that you pronounced. The teacher may also give the drill as a test of your ability to distinguish between back vowels.

1. (a. cat)(b. cot) Would you call it a _____?
2. (a. shack)(b. shock) He had a _____ in the woods.
3. (a. map)(b. mop) You can't clean that floor with a _____.
4. (a. far)(b. fur) Is it _____ from the zoo?
5. (a. doll)(b. dull) She's wearing a _____ hat.
6. (a. bomb)(b. bum) One _____ can cause a lot of damage.
7. (a. barn)(b. burn) Take good care of that _____.
8. (a. lock)(b. luck) We depend on our _____ to avoid burglars.
9. (a. hall)(b. whole) Shall we paint the _____ floor?
10. (a. naught)(b. note) I wrote a _____ on

the slip of paper.
11. (a. cost)(b. coast) The _____ is high along the shore.
12. (a. faun)(b. phone) Do you have a _____ in your study?
13. (a. awed)(b. owed) The speaker _____ every man there.
14. (a. horse)(b. hearse) He went to the funeral on a _____ .
15. (a. balks)(b. bucks) The pony _____ badly.
16. (a. boat)(b. boot) I'm sure such a _____ will float.
17. (a. foal)(b. fool) She loves that _____ dearly.
18. (a. took)(b. tuck) I _____ the money in my pocket.
19. (a. pull)(b. pool) To have no _____ is a misfortune in Hollywood.
20. (a. school)(b. skull) A _____ can teach many lessons.

If facilities are available, it should be most instructive to record the above drill. You might make notes of the word you intend to use in each sentence: 1-a, 2-b, 3-b, etc. Then record, following your notes, and put the latter away where you cannot see them for several days. After an interval long enough to allow yourself to forget which word you used in each sentence, listen to the recording and write down what you hear. Finally, compare your original notes with the record of what you later heard. You might also have another student listen to your record and make notes of what he hears. Did you in every case hear the word you originally intended to use? Did the other student always hear the same word you heard? Are you now making your back vowels with enough clarity to be understood regularly?

J. Read these sentences aloud, making as clear a distinction as possible between the vowels of the words in italics:

1. A *black* cat *blocked* my way.
2. His story only *adds* to the *oddness* of what happened.
3. You'll be *hot* without a *hat*.
4. The sea is *becoming* *calm*.
5. It fell *suddenly* on the *sod*.
6. The *ducks* swim under the *dock*.
7. We heard a *shot* and *shut* the door.

8. I think he *heard*, though he's *hard* of hearing.
9. When they *woke*, they took a *walk*.
10. Every man brought his own *bowling ball*.
11. I *saw* her *sew* it.
12. The tiger's *claws closed*.
13. It was a noisy *war* of *words*.
14. All was *done* before *dawn*.
15. I *stole* up behind the *stool*.
16. The results will be *known* by *noon*.
17. We made a *rush* for the *bushes*.
18. The child has *good blood*.
19. He just *stood* and looked at his *food*.
20. Soon the *sun* will come out.

K. All the sentences in each of the following groups have the same rhythm and intonation. Sentence stresses are marked. Go through each group several times until you can produce that particular pattern rapidly and smoothly:

1. a. The bíll has góne to Cóngress.
   b. The Sénate hásn't pássed it.
   c. The séssion's néarly óver.
   d. Deláy would cáuse us tróuble.
   e. We néed to knów the réason.

2. a. Spríng is the prélude to súmmer.
   b. Whát is the náme of the áctor?
   c. Róbert is táller than yóu are.
   d. Whén is the lády expécted?
   e. Whó has the cóurage to trý it?

3. a. The inflátion may léad to a depréssion.
   b. It's a fáshion I réad of in the pápers.
   c. I can gíve you the ánswer in a mínute.
   d. I'll repéat the remárk just as I héard it.
   e. You can sée in a móment that he néeds it.

4. a. When the cát's awáy, the míce will pláy.
   b. If the príce is ríght, I'll búy the cár.
   c. Though the níghts are cóld, it's wárm todáy.
   d. As you súrely knów, it's tíme for lúnch.
   e. Since he séems surprísed, you'd bétter spéak.

L. Read aloud several pages of English, concentrating your attention on the correct formation of the back vowel with which you have most difficulty.

LESSON XII

"Long" and "Short" Vowels

I. The Theory of "Long" and "Short" Vowels.

Lessons X and XI were designed to help you avoid that type of vowel substitution which is due to inability to hear or reproduce clearly an English vowel which does not exist as a distinctive sound or is formed differently in your mother tongue. This lesson and the one following are aimed at the other type of difficulty students may have in giving the stressed vowel of a word its correct value: vowel substitutions caused by the inconsistencies of English spelling, or the differences between the English and some other system of spelling. In order to approach the problem, we must examine such relationships as may exist between vowel sounds and the way they are ordinarily spelled.

For many years a great many beginning English grammars in various countries of the world have taught the theory of "long" and "short" vowels. This is also the theory behind the system of diacritical marks used in many of our dictionaries: a straight line is placed over "long" vowels, as in lāte; a curved line over "short" vowels, as in păt.

In its simplest form, the theory is that each of the five English vowels — a, e, i, o, u — has two most common sounds in stressed syllables, a "long" sound and a "short" sound:

LETTER	LONG SOUND	SHORT SOUND
a	[e], lāte	[æ], păt
e	[i], ēve	[ɛ], ĕnd
i	[ɑɪ], īce	[ɪ], sĭt
o	[o], ōld	[ɑ], ŏdd
u	[yu], cūbe	[ə], ŭp

(y, as a vowel, usually sounds like "long" i, [ɑɪ]).

Each vowel is pronounced with its "long" sound,

1. If it is final in the syllable:
   pā-per, shē, fī-nal, nō, dū-ty

2. If it is followed by an unpronounced e, or a consonant plus an unpronounced e:
   māke, ēve, dīe, Pōe, ūse

Each vowel is pronounced with its "short" sound,
1. If it is followed in the same syllable by a consongnt:
   măt-ter, wĕnt, rĭv-er, dŏc-tor, cŭt

It should be remembered that these "rules" apply only to vowels in *stressed* syllables; we already know that, when *unstressed*, almost all vowels are pronounced [ə] or [ɪ].

II. Stressed Vowels Followed by a Consonant, Then by Another Vowel Sound.

One limitation of the theory is that it does not explain clearly the pronunciation of the vowels in words like *ever* and *even*, where the stressed vowel is followed by a consonant and then by another vowel sound. Is the e of ever in a "long" or "short" position; is it final in the syllable or followed in the same syllable by a consonant? In other words, is the v a part of the first syllable or the second? If v is the last sound in the first syllable, then the e is in a "short" position and should be pronounced [ɛ̆]; if v is part of the second syllable, e is in a "long" position and should be pronounced as [ī]. But how can a student know where the syllables of the word are to be divided? If he looks up the rules for the division of syllables, he will find that a consonant between two vowel sounds, such as the v in ever, goes with the first syllable if the preceding vowel is "short," and with the second syllable if the preceding vowel is "long". This information, of course, leads him in a vicious circle and is useless unless the student already knows how to pronounce the e of ever. The theory of long and short vowels could not have helped him to determine the pronunciation of an unknown word of the type of ever and even. He must simply learn that ever is pronounced [ɛ̆v-ər], and even [ī-vən].

Actually, the situation with regard to words of this kind — in which the stressed vowel is followed by a consonant and then by another vowel sound — varies with each vowel. In common words of this type (but not necessarily in uncommon, learned words):

i almost always has its "short" sound:

American English Pronunciation

SHORT	LONG
city [sɪ́tɪ]	final [fáɪnḷ]
condition [kəndɪ́ʃən]	
continue [kəntɪ́nyə]	
figure [fɪ́gyər]	
finish [fɪ́nɪʃ]	
given [gɪ́vən]	
minute [mɪ́nɪt]	
river [rɪ́vər]	
spirit [spɪ́rɪt]	
visit [vɪ́zɪt]	

<u>e</u> has its "long" sound more often than <u>i</u> does, but the "short" sound is still much more frequent than the "long" one:

SHORT	LONG
American [əmɛ́rɪkən]	equal [íkwəl]
enemy [ɛ́nəmɪ]	even [ívən]
ever [ɛ́vər]	
general [dʒɛ́nərəl]	
necessary [nɛ́səsɛ́rɪ]	
never [nɛ́vər]	
present [prɛ́zənt]	
second [sɛ́kənd]	
seven [sɛ́vən]	
together [təgɛ́ðər]	

<u>a</u> has its "long" and "short" sounds with almost equal frequency:

SHORT	LONG
animal [ǽnɪməl]	paper [pépər]
family [fǽməlɪ]	baby [bébɪ]
gather [gǽðər]	famous [fémǝs]
natural [nǽtʃərəl]	favor [févər]
rapid [rǽpɪd]	labor [lébər]
rather [rǽðər]	lady [lédɪ]
travel [trǽvəl]	nation [néʃən]
value [vǽlyə]	nature [nétʃər]
	station [stéʃən]

<u>o</u> has its "long" sound more often than its "short" one:

SHORT	LONG
body [bɑ́dɪ]	broken [brókən]
honor [ɑ́nər]	moment [mómənt]
promise [prɑ́mɪs]	notice [nótɪs]
proper [prɑ́pər]	ocean [óʃən]
	open [ópən]

over [óvər]
story [stóri]

u almost always has its "long" sound:

SHORT

study [stÿdɪ]

LONG

during [dyúrɪŋ]
duty [dyútɪ]
music [myúzɪk]
union [yúnyən]
usual [yúʒwəl]

In other words, if you had to guess at the pronunciation of the i in an unfamiliar word like *tibia*, there would be a greater chance of your being right if you gave the i its "short" sound and said [tíbɪə]. The "short" sound of [ɛ] would be a better guess for the e of *senary* than the "long" sound of [i]. There would be almost equal chances that the a of *manic* should have a "long" or a "short" sound; actually the word may be pronounced either [mḗnɪk] or [mǣnɪk]. It would be safer to give the o of *logy* its "long" sound, [lóʤɪ]; and you could be almost sure that the u of *cuticle* should be pronounced with a "long" [yu].

You may find the above explanation easier to remember if you will note that, in the type of word we have been discussing — where the stressed vowel is followed by a consonant and then by another vowel sound — the letters we associate with front vowels, i and e, tend to have their "short" sound, and the letters we associate with back vowels, o and u, usually have their "long" sound.

III. Limitations and Values of the Theory.

Another limitation, and a very important one, of the theory of "long" and "short" vowels is that a very large number of common words are simply not pronounced according to the rules, and must therefore be thought of as exceptions. For example, the letter i in the "short" position (followed in the same syllable by a consonant) should be pronounced [ɪ], but in practice is pronounced [ɑɪ] almost as frequently: *child* [tʃɑɪld], *kind* [kɑɪnd], *light* [lɑɪt]. If the theory of long and short vowels is to be of value to you, you must keep in mind that its rules merely call attention to tendencies and are less perfect even than many other so-called laws of language. There is a large group of words the pronunciation of which could not be explained by any set of rules, however complicated, and which must therefore be learned individually.

A very large number of vowels are not pronounced according to the theory when they are followed by <u>l</u> or <u>r</u>. Because of the movements made by the speech organs in preparing to pronounce these two consonants, <u>l</u> and <u>r</u> tend to make any vowel which precedes them have more of a back sound than it would normally have. Thus, <u>a</u> in the "short" position is usually pronounced [æ]: *actor* [ǽktər]; but <u>a</u> in the "short" position followed by <u>l</u> is ordinarily pronounced [ɔ]: *alter* [ɔ́ltər]. And <u>a</u> in the "short" position followed by r usually has the sound of [ɑ]: *arm* [ɑrm].

Table Showing How Vowels Followed by "L" or "R" Vary from the Sound They Should Have According to the Theory of "Long" and "Short" Vowels

IN "LONG" POSITION

<u>a</u>-Normal sound,
  according to theory   [e], l<u>a</u>te [l<u>e</u>t]
  Followed by <u>l</u>   [eə], s<u>a</u>le [s<u>eə</u>l]
  Followed by <u>r</u>   [ɛə], c<u>a</u>re [k<u>ɛə</u>r]

IN "SHORT" POSITION

Normal sound,
  according to theory   [æ], s<u>a</u>t [s<u>æ</u>t]
  Followed by <u>l</u>   [ɔ], <u>a</u>lter [ɔ́ltər]
  Followed by <u>r</u>   [ɑ], c<u>a</u>r [k<u>ɑ</u>r]

IN "LONG" POSITION

<u>e</u>-Normal sound,
  according to theory   [i], <u>e</u>ven [<u>i</u>vən]
  Followed by <u>l</u>   (not common)
  Followed by <u>r</u>   [ɪə], h<u>e</u>re [h<u>ɪə</u>r]

IN "SHORT" POSITION

Normal sound,
  according to theory   [ɛ], m<u>e</u>t [m<u>ɛ</u>t]
  Followed by <u>l</u>   [ɛə], w<u>e</u>ll [w<u>ɛə</u>l]
  Followed by <u>r</u>   [ə], v<u>e</u>rb [v<u>ə</u>rb]

IN "LONG" POSITION

<u>i</u>-Normal sound,
  according to theory   [ɑɪ], m<u>i</u>ne [m<u>ɑɪ</u>n]
  Followed by <u>l</u>   (same)
  Followed by <u>r</u>   (same)

IN "SHORT" POSITION

Normal sound,
  according to theory   [ɪ], h<u>i</u>t [h<u>ɪ</u>t]
  Followed by <u>l</u>   [ɪə], h<u>i</u>ll [h<u>ɪə</u>l]

Followed by r	[ə], sir [sər]

IN "LONG" POSITION

o-Normal sound, according to theory	[o], rose [roz]
Followed by l	(same)
Followed by r	(same)

IN "SHORT" POSITION

Normal sound, according to theory	[a], hot [hat]
Followed by l	[o], cold [kold]
Followed by r	[ɔ], for [fɔr]

u- (No variation)

    A third limitation of the theory of "long" and "short" vowels is that the terms it uses are not scientifically accurate, in the sense that more time is frequently taken in forming so-called "short" vowels than in forming "long" ones. The words "short" and "long" should mean that "short" vowels require less time to pronounce than "long" ones. Yet the "long" e of beat [bit] is a shorter sound than the "short" i of bid [brːd]. In the sentence "His name is John", the "short" o of John is surely longer than the "long" a of name. The vowel of bid is long because it is followed by a voiced consonant, and that of beat is short because followed by a voiceless consonant (see Lesson VIII, Section II). In the particular sentence cited above, the o of John is unusually long because it must be pronounced on both the high and low tones of the intonation pattern (see Lesson V, Section II).

    In spite of its limitations, however, the theory of "long" and "short" vowels is the most successful attempt which has yet been made to explain, logically and with relative simplicity, the relationship between the spelling and the sounds of English vowels. In view of the large number of pronunciation errors which even advanced students of English make because of their lack of clear associations between vowel sounds and their usual spelling, it is worth your while to familiarize yourself with the theory, or renew your acquaintance with it. You will then be in a position to identify words of irregular pronunciation more easily, and to concentrate on learning them individually.

    The theory should also be a help to you in the troublesome problem of dividing words by a hyphen at the end of a line of writing. Remember that "long" vowels usually end a syllable (except when followed by a consonant plus a silent e), but short vowels do not.

If you happen to know how the first vowel in *finish* [fɪnɪʃ] and *final* [faɪnḷ] is pronounced, you can be sure that the n of *finish* goes with the first syllable, *fin-ish;* and that the n of *final* goes with the second, *fi-nal.*

IV. Exercises.

A. 1. What English vowel sounds do not exist in your mother tongue?
2. In your mother tongue, is it possible to find two words of different meaning exactly alike in sound, except that one contains an [i] and the other an [ɪ] (such as *seat* [sit] and *sit* [sɪt] in English)? Do [e] and [ɛ] ever constitute the only difference between two words? [ɛ] and [æ]? [æ] and [ɑ]? [ɔ] and [o]? [ə] and [ɑ]?
3. Which English vowels and diphthongs do you have most difficulty in pronouncing?
4. Do you sometimes make the mistake of pronouncing *up* as [ap] instead of [əp]? Why? (See Lesson X, Section I.) Do you ever confuse [ʊ] and [ə]? Why? Did you ever mispronounce *post* as [past] instead of [post]; *wash* as [wæʃ] instead of [wɑʃ]? If so, can you explain the reason for the mispronunciation?

B. 1. What are the "long" and "short" sounds of a, e, i, o, and u?
2. According to the theory, should the *stressed* vowel in the following words be "long" or "short?"

a. age	g. cent	m. I	s. doctor
b. ask	h. complete	n. nine	t. go
c. escape	i. expect	o. tie	u. suppose
d. happen	j. less	p. which	v. just
e. lake	k. see	q. bone	w. number
f. be	l. begin	r. box	x. use

Are all 24 of the above words actually pronounced according to the theory?
3. Which of the following very common words have stressed vowels which are *not* pronounced according to the theory of "long" and "short" vowels as explained in this lesson?

a. any	e. busy	i. have	m. only
b. blue	f. give	j. hundred	n. other
c. both	g. glass	k. move	o. pure
d. bottom	h. gone	l. no	p. put

              q. race   s. then   u. was   w. water
              r. sing   t. these   v. watch   x. wrong
C. What would be the safest guess as to the vowel
   sound in the stressed syllable of each of these
   words (see Section II of this lesson)?
     1. facet   5. hobo   9. mucous   13. penicil
     2. fetus   6. hymic   10. nematode 14. ribald
     3. focal   7. manor   11. nicotine 15. rosin
     4. Hades   8. mimic   12. pagan   16. sesame
   Look up each word in a good pronouncing dictionary and see how often you guessed correctly.

D. Pronounce several times the following pairs of
   words, and notice how the presence of an l or r
   changes the sound of the vowel in each case
   (see Section III of this lesson):
     1. cat-cart   10. mane-male   18. fist-first
     2. had-hard   11. gem-germ   19. sick-silk
     3. case-care   12. beg-berg   20. sit-silt
     4. date-dare   13. ten-tern   21. spot-sport
     5. bad-bald   14. mete-mere   22. stock-stork
     6. sat-salt   15. met-melt   23. cod-cold
     7. back-balk   16. sped-spelled 24. God-gold
     8. after-alter   17. bid-bird   25. cot-colt
     9. save-sale
   Write the phonetic symbol which represents the
   vowel of each word.

E. 1. Keeping in mind that long vowels usually
      end syllables and short vowels do not, di-
      vide these words into syllables:
        a. bacon   e. metal   i. promise   m. rival
        b. frozen   f. motor   j. punish   n. second
        c. gather   g. notion   k. pupil   o. table
        d. mason   h. pity   l. risen   p. together

   2. Why do you suppose the final p of hop is
      doubled when -ing is added? Why double the g
      of big when -est is added? Why double the b
      of rob when -ed is added?

F. Let the members of the class ask and answer
   questions about their school work. As they
   speak, the instructor should listen carefully
   and encourage them to diphthongize [e] and [o]
   slightly in cases where such diphthongization
   would be most natural: when the vowel is final,
   when it is followed by a final voiced consonant,
   or when it is pronounced with an inflection at
   the end of an intonation pattern (see Lesson X,
   Section IV). Key expressions for use in the
   questions might be: *grade, raise your grade,
   call the roll, every day, an " A," know, fail,*

say, study load, closed section, go, at home, alone, show, loathe, what page, change sections, study aids.

G. Work on the following passage for naturalness of intonation and rhythm. After you have prepared it carefully, this material may be recorded.

1. "Hello", he said. 2. She pushed her glasses up onto her forehead as he kissed her. 3. "Listen, Marge, I don't want us to get our wires crossed. 4. I've made a date with Eddie to go fishing next Monday. 5. It's the opening of the season, so put that down in your book, will you?" 6. She looked at her engagement pad.

7. "Oh, Joe! But that's the night we dine with the Medfords, darling." 8. "Oh, oh!" he said, "I knew there'd be a snag. 9. Have you accepted already?" 10. "Yes," she said, "of course."

11. "What do you mean 'of course'?" he said.

12. "Why on earth couldn't you have asked me about it, eh? 13. Then I'd have told you to

keep the fifteenth clear."

(Adapted from the story "A Matter of Pride." by Christopher La Farge, originally published in *The New Yorker*.)

H. Outside of class prepare several pages of a magazine article for reading aloud by marking the pauses by means of which it can best be divided into thought groups. Then read the article, being careful to blend your words together within thought groups. Try to avoid glottal stops and finishing sounds (see Lesson IV, Section IV).

LESSON XIII

Spelling and Vowel Sounds

I. The Relationship Between Spelling and Sound.

This lesson is an amplification of the fundamental material presented in Lesson XII. The most important relationships between the spelling and pronunciation of stressed vowels in English words are the result of the vowel's being in a "long" or "short" position, or of its being followed by an l or r. But it seems worthwhile to know also about certain other relationships of less general application: for example, the combination ea, which is normally pronounced [i] as in *each*, usually has the sound of [ɛ] before a d — *bread, dead, head*.

Facts of this nature are included in the long table which follows. You are not expected to memorize the table. The exercises at the end of the lesson will help you to become familiar with it, and you may wish to refer to it later. It should be of help to you in your attempts to avoid that type of vowel substitution which is caused by the way in which a word is spelled.

Of course, it will never be possible to explain logically, by a neat set of rules, the spelling of *all* English vowel sounds. You will find that in some cases the exceptions are almost as numerous as the examples on which a "rule" is based. You should know of such relationships as do exist between sound and spelling, but you should also realize that even the clearest of these cannot always be trusted. In the final analysis, the pronunciation of many words must simply be learned individually. Pay particular attention to the exceptions listed below!

II. The Pronunciation of Stressed Vowels.

Vowel Combination	Pronunciation	Examples	Common Exceptions
1. a, in "long" position, normally	[e]	face [fes], brave [brev], shape [ʃep], take [tek]	have [hæv] or [hev]; water [wɔ́tɚ]; father [fɑ́ðɚ]
2. a, in "long" position, before r	[ee]	sale [seel], male [meel], pale [peel], whale [hweel]	
3. a, in "long" position, before r	[eə]	care [keər], square [skweər], dare [deər], rare [reər]	[ɑr] or [ær]
4. a, in "short" position, normally	[æ]	ask [æsk], man [mæn], sad [sæd], chance [tʃæns], bank [bæŋk], last [læst], pass [pæs], bag [bæg], path [pæθ], sand [sænd], fancy [fǽnsɪ], master [mǽstɚ]	able [ébəl], table [tébəl], change [tʃendʒ], strange [strendʒ]; taste [test], waste [west]; want [wɑnt], watch [wɑtʃ], what [hwɑt], wash [wɑʃ], was [wɑz] or [wʌz], any [ɛ́nɪ], many [mɛ́nɪ]
5. a, in "short" position, before l	[ɔ]	all [ɔl], salt [sɔlt], ball [bɔl], call [kɔl]	half [hæf], shall [ʃæl]
6. a, in "short" position, before r	[ɑ]	art [ɑrt], star [stɑr], car [kɑr], charge [tʃɑrdʒ]	quarter [kwɔ́rtɚ], warm [wɔrm], war [wɔr]
7. ai, normally	[e]	plain [plen], raise [rez], wait [wet], paint [pent]	again [əgén] or [əgén], said [sɛd]
8. ai, before l	[ee]	sail [seel], tail [teel], mail [meel], fail [feel]	

1. In many parts of the United States, -are and -air are pronounced [ær] instead of [eə].

American English Pronunciation

(Vowel Combination)	(Pronunciation)	(Examples)	(Common Exceptions)
9. <u>ai</u>, before <u>r</u>	[ɛə]¹	air [ɛə], chair [tʃɛə] hair [hɛə], fair [fɛə]	
10. <u>au</u>	[ɔ]	cause [kɔz], pause [pɔz] Paul [pɔl], daughter [dɔtɚ]	laugh [læf]
11. <u>aw</u>	[ɔ]	draw [drɔ], law [lɔ] saw [sɔ], paw [pɔ]	
12. <u>ay</u>	[e]	say [se], stay [ste] ways [wez], day [de]	says [sɛz]
13. <u>e</u>, in "long" position, normally	[i]	be [bi], he [hi], she [ʃi] these [ðiz], even [ivən]	
14. <u>e</u>, in "long" position, before <u>r</u>	[ɪr]	here [hɪr], mere [mɪr] sincere [sɪnsɪr], sphere [sfɪr]	there [ðɛə], where [hwɛə] were [wɚ]
15. <u>e</u>, in "short" position, normally	[ɛ]	best [bɛst], dress [drɛs] end [ɛnd], fence [fɛns]	pretty [prɪti]
16. <u>e</u>, in "short" position, before <u>l</u>	[ɛə]	bell [bɛəl], else [ɛəls] help [hɛəp], twelve [twɛəlv]	
17. <u>e</u>, in "short" position, before <u>r</u>	[ɚ]	her [hɚ], serves [sɚvz] verb [vɚb], perfect [pɚfɪkt]	
18. <u>ea</u>, normally	[i]	each [itʃ], leave [liv] mean [min], please [pliz] reach [ritʃ], sea [si]	break [brek], great [gret]; breakfast [brɛkfəst], heaven [hɛvən], heavy [hɛvi].

---

1. In many parts of the United States, *-are* and *-air* are pronounced [ɛr] instead of [ɛə].

132

Spelling and Vowel Sounds

(Vowel Combination)	(Pronunciation)	(Examples)	(Common Exceptions)
19. ea, before d	[e]	speak [spik], beast [bist], heat [hit], stream [strim], teach [tit͡ʃ], weak [wik]	measure [mɛ́ʒər], pleasant [plɛ́zənt], pleasure [plɛ́ʒər], death [dɛθ], weather [wɛ́ðər]
20. ea, before l	[ei]	bread [brɛd], dead [dɛd], head [hɛd], ready [rɛ́di]	bead [bid], lead (verb) [lid], read (present tense) [rid]
		pay [pei], steal [stiel]	health [hɛlθ]
21. ea, before r, normally	[ɛr]	clear [klɪr], dear [dɪr], ear [ɪr], hear [hɪr]	bear [bɛər], tear (rip) [tɛər], wear [wɛər]
22. ea, before r, and another consonant	[ə]	early [ə́ri], earth [ərθ], learn [lərn], heard [hərd]	heart [hart]
23. ee, normally	[i]	deep [dip], feet [fit], free [fri], green [grin]	been [bɪn]
24. ee, before l	[ie]	feel [fiel], wheel [hwiel], heel [hiel], steel [stiel]	
25. ee, before r	[ɛr]	beer [brɛr], cheer [t͡ʃɛr], deer [dɛr]	
26. ei, normally	[i]	either [íðər], receive [rɪsív], seize [siz]	veil [veɪ], their [ðɛər]
27. ei, before g or n	[eː]	eight [et], neighbor [nébər], weigh [we], reign [ren], rein [ren], vein [ven]	height [haɪt]
28. ew.	[yu]	few [fyu], new [nyu]	grew [gru]

American English Pronunciation

(Vowel Combination)	(Pronunciation)	(Examples)	(Common Exceptions)
29. ey	[e]	they [ðe], convey [kənve]	eye [aɪ]
30. i. in "long" position	[aɪ]	die [daɪ], lie [laɪ], drive [draɪv], arrive [əraɪv]	give [gɪv], live (verb) [lɪv], iron [aɪərn]
31. i. in "short" position, normally	[ɪ]	big [bɪg], sing [sɪŋ], fish [fɪʃ], since [sɪns]	sign [saɪn], island [aɪlənd]
32. i. in "short" position, before gh, ld (final), or nd (final)	[aɪ]	high [haɪ], night [naɪt]; child [tʃaɪld], wild [waɪld]; wind (verb) [waɪnd], find [faɪnd], mind [maɪnd]	wind (noun) [wɪnd]
33. i. in "short" position, before l	[ɪ]	ill [ɪl], milk [mɪlk], until [əntɪl]	
34. i. in "short" position, before r	[ɜ]	bird [bɜrd], first [fɜrst], girl [gɜrl]	
35. ie. normally	[i]	chief [tʃif], believe [bɪliv], piece [pis], grief [grif]	friend [frɛnd]; also see i in "long" position.
36. ie. before l	[i]	field [fild], yield [jild]	
37. ie. before r	[ɪr]	pier [pɪr], fierce [fɪrs]	
38. o. in "long" position	[o]	go [go], no [no], so [so]; ago [əgo], alone [əlon]; close (verb) [kloz], home [hom], hope [hop], more [mor]; stone [ston], those [ðoz], whole [hol], bone [bon]	do [du], into [ɪntu], to [tu]; or [ɔr], two [tu], who [hu]; move [muv], lose [luz]; prove [pruv], whose [huz]; gone [gɔn], does [dʌz]; shoe [ʃu], above [əbʌv]

(Vowel Combination)	(Pronunciation)	(Examples)	(Common Exceptions)
39. o, in "short" position, before a stop	[a]	nose [noz], note [not], shore [ʃor], smoke [smok], spoke [spok], suppose [səpoz]	
40. o, in "short" position, before a continuant, normally	[ɔ]	box [baks], drop [drap], God [gad], got [gat], rock [rak], log [lag]. across [əkrɔs], corn [kɔrn], cross [krɔs], for [fɔr], form [fɔrm], long [lɔŋ], loss [lɔs], lost [lɔst], moth [mɔθ], north [nɔrθ], off [ɔf], soft [sɔft], storm [stɔrm], strong [strɔŋ], wrong [rɔŋ], forth [fɔrθ], report [rɪpɔrt], morning [mɔrnɪŋ], often [ɔfən], order [ɔrdər], former [fɔrmər], office [ɔfɪs], tomorrow [təmɔro]. born [bɔrn], belong [bɪlɔŋ], cloth [klɔθ], cost [kɔst], lord [lɔrd], song [sɔŋ]	come [kʌm], love [lʌv], none [nʌn], done [dʌn], some [sʌm], one [wʌn]. mother [mʌðər], nothing [nʌθɪŋ], discover [dɪskʌvər], other [ʌðər], cover [kʌvər], color [kʌlər], brother [brʌðər], another [ənʌðər], son [sʌn], front [frʌnt], tongue [tʌŋ], company [kʌmpənɪ], among [əmʌŋ], month [mʌnθ], wonder [wʌndər], only [onlɪ], don't [dont], both [boθ], most [most], post [post], follow [falo], hollow [halo], plow [plaw], prow [praw]. worth [wɝθ], know [no], possible [pasɪbəl], common [kamən], once [wʌns], whom [hum], woman [wʊmən], women [wɪmɪn]
41. o, in "short" position, before l	[o]	cold [kold], roll [rol], told [told], soldier [soldʒər]	

American English Pronunciation

(Vowel Combination)	(Pronunciation)	(Examples)	(Common Exceptions)
42. oa	[o]	board [bord], boat [bot], coal [kol], coast [kost]	broad [brɔd]
43. oi	[ɔi]	point [pɔint], voice [vɔis], noise [nɔiz], soil [sɔil]	
44. oo, final	[u]	too [tu], woo [wu]	
45. oo, before a before a stop	[ʊ]	hood [hʊd], stood [stʊd], good [gʊd], wood [wʊd], book [bʊk], brook [brʊk], cook [kʊk], hook [hʊk], look [lʊk], shook [ʃʊk], took [tʊk], coop [kup], foot [fʊt], soot [sʊt]	blood [blʌd], flood [flʌd], food [fud], droop [drup], loop [lup], stoop [stup], troop [trup], boot [but], root [rut], shoot [ʃut]
46. oo, before a continuant, normally	[u]	room [rum], school [skul], soon [sun], moon [mun]	
47. oo, before r	[o]	door [dor], floor [flor]	poor [pur]
48. ou, normally	[aʊ]	about [əbaʊt], around [əraʊnd], found [faʊnd], house [haʊs], out [aʊt], sound [saʊnd], south [saʊθ], cloud [klaʊd], count [kaʊnt], doubt [daʊt], loud [laʊd], mouth [maʊθ]	brought [brɔt], thought [θɔt], though [ðo], although [ɔlðo], through [θru], you [yu], country [kʌntri], double [dʌbəl], touch [tʌtʃ], young [yʌŋ], trouble [trʌbəl]
49. ou, before l or r, normally	[o]	soul [sol], shoulder [ʃoldər]	your [yʊr], journey [dʒɝni]

(Vowel Combination)	(Pro-nunci-ation)	(Examples)	(Common Exceptions)
50. **ou** before final **ld**	[ʊ]	could [kʊd], should [ʃʊd], would [wʊd].	our [aʊr], hour [aʊr]
51. **ow**	[o] or [aʊ]	bow (weapon, or knot) [bo], blow [blo], flow [flo], grow [gro], know [no], low [lo], own [on], row (line, or to propel with oars) [ro], show [ʃo], slow [slo], snow [sno], throw [θro], toward [tord]; bow (point of boat, or to incline) [baʊ], allow [əlaʊ], down [daʊn], brown [braʊn], how [haʊ], now [naʊ], cow [kaʊ], row (disturbance) [raʊ], crowd [kraʊd], town [taʊn], crown [kraʊn], flower [flaʊr].	
52. **oy**	[ɔɪ]	boy [bɔɪ], destroy [dɪstrɔ́ɪ], joy [dʒɔɪ], toy [tɔɪ].	
53. **u** in "long" position	[yu]	use [yuz], pure [pyʊr], during [dyúrɪŋ], music [myúzɪk]	rule [rul]; blue [blu]
54. **u** in "short" position	[ə]	but [bət], bun [bən], bus [bəs], hut [hət], hup [həp], dump [dəmp], jump [dʒəmp], rush [rəʃ], run [rən].	busy [bɪ́zi]; truth [truθ]; full [fʊl], pull [pʊl], put [pʊt], sugar [ʃʊ́gər].

(Vowel Combination)	(Pronunciation)	(Examples)	(Common Exceptions)
(Other common words in which u has an unusual sound: guard [gɑrd]; build [bɪld]; buy [baɪ]; fruit [frut], suit [sut].)			
55. y	[aɪ]	by [baɪ], fly [flaɪ], cry [kraɪ], sky [skaɪ], supply [səplaɪ]	

III. Exercises.

A. 1. Try to add one new example of your own to illustrate each of the 55 vowel combinations in the preceding table.

2. Each of the following words also is an example of one of the 55 combinations. Give the number of the combination illustrated by each word:

a. set	n. cede	z. boss	al. may
b. hid	o. name	aa. ale	am. lean
c. oats	p. pierce	ab. moo	an. crook
d. call	q. seal	ac. stew	ao. five
e. fare	r. toil	ad. rain	ap. caught
f. cool	s. farm	ae. blind	aq. not
g. fold	t. freight	af. cute	ar. near
h. melt	u. peel	ag. search	as. fourth
i. peer	v. proud	ah. deceive	at. verse
j. shield	w. sincere	ai. spread	au. piece
k. lawn	x. pair	aj. such	av. nail
l. hat	y. third	ak. meet	aw. store
m. fill			

B. Do for all the vowel sounds as has been done for [i] below; that is, rearrange the long table given in this lesson so as to show all the different ways in which each stressed vowel sound is commonly spelled. Fill in as many as possible of the spelling combinations from memory before referring back to the table.

Usual Ways of Spelling the Stressed Vowel Sounds

SOUND	COMBINATION	EXAMPLE
1. [i]	a. e, "long", normally	be
	b. ea, normally	each
	c. ee, normally	deep
	d. ei, normally	seize
	e. ie, normally	chief
2. [ɪ]	a.	
3. [e]	a.	
	b.	
	c.	
	d.	
	e.	
4. [ɛ]	a.	
	b.	
5. [æ]	a.	

American English Pronunciation

6. [ɑ]   a. _____
         b. _____

7. [ɔ]   a. _____
         b. _____
         c. _____
         d. _____

8. [o]   a. _____
         b. _____
         c. _____
         d. _____
         e. _____
         f. _____

9. [ʊ]   a. _____
         b. _____

10. [u] a. _____
         b. _____

11. [ə] a. _____
         b. _____
         c. _____
         d. _____

12. [iə] a. _____
         b. _____
         c. _____

13. [ɪə] a. _____
         b. _____
         c. _____
         d. _____
         e. _____

14. [eə] a. _____
         b. _____

15. [ɛə] a. _____
         b. _____
         c. _____

16. [yu] a. _____
         b. _____

17. [ɑɪ] a. _____
         b. _____
         c. _____

18. [ɑʊ] a. _____
         b. _____

19. [ɔɪ] a. _____
         b. _____

C. You may not be familiar with most of the following words, but all are pronounced regularly according to the rules formulated in this lesson. How should each be pronounced? Remember that the rules cited in the long table refer only to *stressed* vowels. You already know (Lesson III) the sounds usually given to unstressed vowels.

1. ábbacy	14. tread	27. wince	39. cajóle
2. sparse	15. streak	28. tithe	40. loft
3. scald	16. earl	29. hind	41. thong
4. smalt	17. yearn	30. rind	42. wọld
5. taut	18. hearse	31. besmirch	43. bólster
6. paunch	19. weald	32. dirge	44. rook
7. abele	20. blear	33. filch	45. bourn
8. subvene	21. drear	34. frieze	46. slouch
9. absterge	22. veer	35. fiend	47. pounce
10. pert	23. deign	36. wield	48. bulge
11. mércurate	24. skein	37. tier	49. spume
12. sere	25. askew	38. stooge	50. rebuke
13. delve	26. abeyance		

D. The words in the list below are all exceptions to our list of rules. Be sure you know exactly what sound should be given to the stressed vowel in each of them; look them up in a pronouncing dictionary if necessary. Then identify the rule to which each is an exception:

1. pear	6. ninth	11. award	16. deaf
2. calm	7. swamp	12. beard	17. bull
3. doll	8. Tom	13. plead	18. glove
4. scoop	9. machine	14. youth	19. ceil
5. realm	10. foul	15. aunt	20. key

E. Write the phonetic symbol which represents the vowel sound in each of these exceptional words. Then read the entire list several times.

1. do	15. stone	29. worth	43. other
2. go	16. bone	30. north	44. cover
3. move	17. done	31. most	45. over
4. stove	18. does	32. cost	46. govern
5. above	19. shoes	33. post	47. clover
6. prove	20. foes	34. lost	48. blood
7. love	21. both	35. wonder	49. good
8. wove	22. cloth	36. ponder	50. food
9. lose	23. come	37. among	51. wood
10. those	24. home	38. long	52. flood
11. whose	25. some	39. son	53. boot
12. nose	26. dome	40. on	54. foot
13. none	27. word	41. mother	55. root
14. gone	28. lord	42. bother	56. soot

57. blow   59. flow   61. grown   63. crown
58. how   60. cow   62. town   64. own

F. The sentences in each of the following groups have the same rhythm and intonation. Sentence stresses are marked. Repeat each group until you can produce that particular pattern rapidly and smoothly. (This material is suitable for recording.)

1.
   a. To tell us to be quiet is unreasonable.
   b. The owner is prepared to redecorate it.
   c. I'll help you with your coat when you're ready for it.
   d. I think he would be shocked if you asked him for it.
   e. I never would have thought you would give it to me.

2.
   a. Have you studied your lessons?
   b. Does he speak with an accent?
   c. Is it wrong to get angry?
   d. Are you willing to tell me?
   e. Can you ever believe it?

3.
   a. I have exams in mathematics and chemistry.
   b. I would have thought it was a Packard or Cadillac.
   c. Was he identified beforehand or afterward?
   d. You'll have to promise me to love it and cherish it.
   e. Do you prefer to have it toasted or untoasted?

4.
   a. With a new car and enough time we could make it.
   b. It's a long time since he left home for the city.
   c. If you can't go, you can write now and explain it.
   d. When the war ends and the peace comes, we'll be happy.
   e. There's a fine current of cool air near the window.

G. The intonation patterns marked in for the sentences below are *not natural*. In fact, each sentence represents a type of "intonation error" often made by students. What suggestions could you make to help a person who used such patterns improve his speech?

1. How are you, Mr. Williams?

2. It's a long way, isn't it?

3. You can't be patient forever.

4. What do you want with a dictionary?

5. How are you feeling this morning?

6. I think it's prettier over there, John.

7. It's the center of our thoughts, our hopes, and our fears.

8. He won't do a thing to help.

H. Outside of class prepare several pages of a short story for reading aloud by finding and underscoring all syllabic consonants (see Lesson IX, Section III). Then read the material with attention focused on the words you have marked.

LESSON XIV

Consonant Substitutions: I

I. Consonant Substitutions.

You should be familiar by now with the idea of vowel substitutions, and will probably understand immediately what is meant by the similar phrase, "consonant substitutions." The latter is, of course, that type of speech error in which an incorrect consonant is used in place of the correct one: the pronunciation of *those* as [doz] instead of [ðoz], of *days* as [des] instead of [dez].

A very large number of such substitutions involve the replacement of a voiced consonant by its voiceless counterpart, or vice versa. We have already treated this type of error in Lessons VII and VIII. In Lessons XIV and XV, which make up the last unit of this manual, we shall work on several common and troublesome consonant substitutions of other kinds, in which the error is not usually due to incorrect voicing. However, a knowledge of the system of consonant classification and the effect an initial or final position may have on a consonant sound — the material of Lessons VII and VIII — is basic in attacking the problem before us.

II. [t] and [θ], [d] and [ð].

The English sounds [θ] and [ð] occur in very few of the other important tongues of the modern world. Naturally, most students of English as a second language have trouble with the two consonants and often try to replace them in conversational speech by other, more familiar sounds. The most frequent substitutes for [θ] and [ð] seem to be [t] and [d], respectively, though [s] and [z] are sometimes heard also. If you will check back for a moment and think of the points of articulation of these six sounds, you will note how close together they all are.

[ð] and [θ], of course, make up a voiced-voiceless

pair. In the formation of both sounds, the tip of the
tongue should be thrust out quite a way between the
upper and lower teeth. To pronounce a perfect [θ], simply put your tongue between your teeth and blow. Watch
in your hand mirror to see how clearly visible the tongue
tip is. For [θ], both initial and final, the air is
forced between the teeth with considerable pressure. In
fact, the sound is merely the noise of this air rushing
out through its narrow passage. For [ð], there is much
less sound of escaping air, the aspiration being
largely replaced by vibration of the vocal cords. Practice with *teeth* [ti̱θ̱] - *teethe* [ti̱ð̱], *thigh* [θ̱aɪ] - *thy*
[ð̱aɪ], and make the contrast as clear as possible.

When [t] is substituted for [θ], as when a Scandinavian or German pronounces *thing* as [ṯɪŋ] in place of
[θ̱ɪŋ], it means that the tip of the speaker's tongue
has merely touched the upper tooth ridge or the back
of the upper teeth instead of being thrust between the
teeth. Exactly the same thing happens when [d] replaces
[ð], as when *the* is pronounced [ḏə] instead of [ð̱ə].
[θ] and [ð] require a little more effort to make than
[t] and [d], since the tongue must move a little farther to produce them. So, you see, it is not only the
native speaker of English who takes the path of least
resistance.

When [s] is substituted for [θ], or [z] for [ð],
as when the traditional stage Frenchman pronounces
think as [s̱ɪŋk] instead of [θ̱ɪŋk], the speaker is making still less effort than the German who used [t] or
[d]. The Frenchman's tongue tip, in forming [s] or [z],
merely approaches the tooth ridge or upper teeth.

All substitutions of this type are extremely easy
to avoid. One merely has to be sure he inserts the tip
of the tongue between the teeth when he says [θ] or
[ð]. [θ] and [ð] can be seen as easily as they can be
heard, and are among the least difficult sounds for a
lip-reader to identify. If you will use your mirror,
you can tell the difference between [θ/ð] and [t/d] or
[s/z] at a glance.

In spite of the ease with which [t] - for - [θ] and
[d] - for - [ð] substitutions can be corrected when the
speaker makes a conscious effort to form them well,
they may continue for years to mark his English as
"foreign-sounding" at times when he is concentrating
on the thought he wishes to express rather than on the
position of his tongue. This kind of error is especially persistent in the short unstressed words of a sentence, where the tendency is to pronounce with as little effort as possible, and where the student from

abroad may even have worked hard training himself to avoid too much clarity. The combinations *of the* and *said that* are good examples. To eliminate incorrect [d]'s when he is un-self-consciously using such phrases, the student may need to make a considerable disciplined effort. Drills such as those of this lesson may help, especially Exercises A-3 and B-3, in which attention is fixed on the formation of a good [ð] or [θ] at the beginning, then gradually transferred to something else. Final and complete elimination, however, will probably require the reading aloud, with attention concentrated on getting the tongue between the teeth for each th, of passages long enough to insure the formation of an unbreakable habit.

III. [dʒ] and [y].

The [dʒ]-for-[y] substitution is most often noted in the speech of students whose mother tongue is Spanish. In Argentina [dʒ] has replaced [y] altogether in words like *yo* and *suya*. In almost all Latin America this substitution can be heard in words spoken with emphasis. By way of contrast, Scandinavians who learn English tend to make the opposite substitution; in a word like *jump*, they are likely to replace [dʒ] by [y], and pronounce [yəmp] instead of [dʒəmp]. Since the manner in which these two consonant sounds are made in English has not yet been explained in this manual, we shall examine them in some detail.

[y] is essentially a very short and completely unstressed [i] or [ɪ] occurring before some other vowel sound. It is also a glide, which means that it is formed, not in a fixed position, but as the organs of speech move from one place to another. It is heard in words like *yet* [yɛt] and *young* [yəŋ]. The tongue assumes the [ɪ]-position: tip touching lightly the back of the lower front teeth, sides touching the upper bicuspids. Then voicing begins as the tongue moves immediately to the next vowel in the word. [y] cannot be very well pronounced alone or separated from the following vowel.

On the other hand, [dʒ] is classified as an affricate. An affricate is a stop (see Lesson VII, Section II), followed by a slow separation of the organs of speech, which makes the last part of the sound a continuant. As the symbol indicates, [dʒ] is a combination of [d] and [ʒ]. It is voiced, as are both the sounds of which it is composed. You may remember that the voiceless counterpart of [ʒ] is [ʃ]. Both [ʒ] and [ʃ] are normally produced by the sound of air rushing through a long shallow channel between the tongue and the hard palate. At the sides, the channel is closed by contact between the sides of the tongue and the tooth ridge. The lips are somewhat protruded and rounded. For the production of [dʒ] the position is similar, except that for a moment at the beginning of the sound, the tongue touches the tooth ridge all around, thus blocking altogether the escape of air. When a little pressure has built up, the tip of the tongue (but not the sides) moves away from the tooth ridge, opening the channel for the outrush of air.

If you compare the descriptions of [dʒ] and [y], you will note that the essential difference is this contact at the beginning of [dʒ] between the tongue and the upper tooth ridge. For [y], no part of the tongue touches the roof of the mouth; only light contacts are made between the tongue tip and lower teeth and the sides of the tongue and the upper bicuspids. Contrast jet [dʒɛt] and yet [yɛt], and keep your tongue away from your palate and tooth ridge for [y].

IV. [ʃ] and [tʃ].

For reasons which need not be explained here, there is a tendency to substitute [ʃ] for [tʃ] in certain positions, even on the part of students whose mother tongue has a [tʃ]-sound. Thus *question* is frequently mispronounced as [kwɛsʃən] instead of [kwɛstʃən] by speakers of various nationalities.

[ʃ] and [tʃ] are the voiceless counterparts of [ʒ] and [dʒ], and are naturally formed in much the same way, described above, as these latter consonants. Only, in the production of [ʃ] and [tʃ] there is more sound of the outrush of air to make up for the lack of voicing. When [ʃ] is substituted for [tʃ], it simply means that the brief contact between the tongue tip and upper tooth ridge, necessary for [t], has been omitted. Compare *sheep* [ʃip] and *cheap* [tʃip], *washer* [waʃər] and *watcher* [watʃər].

V. Exercises.

   A. 1. Listen carefully as your instructor pronounces a prolonged [θ] several times: θ-θ-θ, θ-θ-θ, θ-θ-θ. Imitate his pronunciation of the consonant, making sure you thrust the tip of your tongue between your teeth.

      2. Listen, then imitate as your instructor pronounces the following material. Finally, try to pronounce each word or phrase to his

satisfaction:

a. θɔ
b. θæŋk
c. θɛft
d. θɪŋk
e. θərd
f. θro
g. truθ
h. mənθ
i. ṓθər
j. mɛ́θəd

k. arithmetic
l. thick and thin
m. a thrilling thing
n. beneath his thumb
o. the fourth of the month
p. θɪk - tɪk
q. θim - tim
r. θrɛd - trɛd
s. feeʰ - fet
t. pæθʰ - pæt

u. nə́θɪŋ - nə́tɪŋ
v. ʃiθ - ʃi:ð
w. loθ - lo:ð
x. tiθ - ti:ð
y. íθər - íðər

z. θɪk - sɪk
aa. θæŋk - sæŋk
ab. θəm - səm
ac. mauθ - maus
ad. tɛnθ - tɛns

3. Repeat this drill as rapidly as you can after your instructor. Do not read from the printed page; just imitate what you hear. Each sentence contains at least one [θ], but you should *not* concentrate on these sounds. Think only of the meaning of the sentence. The instructor will tell you if you mispronounce a [θ], and you can try again. The drill is intended to help you begin to make the [θ]-sound well when your attention is directed toward the thought of what you are saying.

    a. I'm thirsty.
    b. I'm thinking hard.
    c. I'm methodical.
    d. I'm very thankful.
    e. I'm through with it.
    f. I'm third in the class.
    g. I'm quite thrilled.
    h. I'm three years older.
    i. I'm thoroughly satisfied.
    j. I'm a thousand miles from home.
    k. I'm always faithful.
    l. I'm not a thief.
    m. I'm having a birthday.
    n. I'm at the theater.
    o. I'm in the bathtub.
    p. I'm going south.
    q. I'm healthily tanned.
    r. I'm losing my teeth.
    s. I'm almost pathetic.
    t. I'm anything you say.

B. (The instructions for Exercise A apply also to this exercise.)
1. ð-ð-ð, ð-ð-ð, ð-ð-ð
2.
   a. ðæn
   b. ðiz
   c. ðɪs
   d. ðɑu
   e. ðəs
   f. suð
   g. brið
   h. lέðər
   i. béðɪŋ
   j. rǽðər

   k. father and mother
   l. smooth feathers
   m. of the weather
   n. get them together
   o. either this or that
   p. ðo - do
   q. ðe - de
   r. ðɛn - dɛn
   s. ðoz - doz
   t. ðɛər - dɛər

   u. tɑɪð - tɑɪd
   v. loð - lod
   w. ʃǽðər - ʃǽdər
   x. wǽrðɪ - wǽrdɪ
   y. ðɑɪ - θʰɑɪ

   z. riːð - riθʰ
   aa. kloð - kloz
   ab. sið - siz
   ac. sɑɪð - sɑɪz
   ad. tið - tiz

3.
   a. You said that you'd rather not.
   b. You said that you'd answer these letters.
   c. You said that you'd be absent this afternoon.
   d. You said that you'd gather up your things.
   e. You said that you'd give clothing.
   f. You said that you'd change those grades.
   g. You said that you'd investigate further.
   h. You said that you'd speak at the beginning of the hour.
   i. You said that you breathed easily.
   j. You said that it bothered you.
   k. You said that you were smothering.
   l. You said that the reverse was the case.
   m. You said that you wouldn't ask this question.
   n. You said that the water was smooth.
   o. You said that you were younger than that.
   p. You said that you liked the idea.
   q. You said that you loathed the place.
   r. You said that you disliked bathing.
   s. You said that you had them already.
   t. You said that they were fun though difficult.

C. 1. Imitate as your teacher pronounces the syllables [dʒo] and [yo] several times. For [dʒo], be sure the tongue touches the tooth ridge; for [yo], avoid such contact carefully.

   2. In the exercise below the same steps may be

carried out as in similar drills done previously: a) the teacher makes sure that the meaning of all words is understood; b) he reads down the columns then across them, and the class imitates his pronunciation; c) the students read across and down, in a group and individually; d) the teacher dictates several words selected at random; e) the students pick out certain words and try to pronounce them so well that the teacher can identify them by letter:

dʒ	y
a. Jew	g. you
b. juice	h. use (noun)
c. jet	i. yet
d. jarred	j. yard
e. joke	k. yoke
f. jail	l. Yale

3. Read these sentences aloud, making as clear a distinction as possible between the [dʒ] and [y] of the underscored words:

a. He has been jeered at for years.
b. You can't make jam with yams.
c. You lie; it was in July.
d. The oranges are juiceless and useless.
e. Please yell when the mixture jells.

D. 1. ʃo, tʃo, ʃo, tʃo, ʃo, tʃo
2.

ʃ	tʃ
a. sheep	g. cheap
b. ship	h. chip
c. shatter	i. chatter
d. mush	j. much
e. mashing	k. matching
f. washer	l. watcher

3. a. The baby shouldn't chew his shoe.
   b. Merchants try to catch all the cash they can.
   c. I never wished to see such a witch.
   d. He uses crutches since his foot was crushed.
   e. You were cheated when you bought that sheet.

E. Your instructor will dictate some of the words from the exercise below for you to recognize and write down. Then you should choose certain of them, not in any fixed order, and try to pronounce them well enough so that he can iden-

tify them. In the phonetic transcription of
each word, marks of length, [ː], and aspiration,
[ʰ], have been added where appropriate (see
Lesson VIII), in order to help you pronounce
more clearly.

1. dead [dɛːd]
2. death [dɛθʰ]
3. debt [dɛt]
4. thread [θʰrɛːd]
5. dread [drɛːd]
6. tread [tʰrɛːd]
7. threat [θʰrɛt]
8. sink [sʰɪŋk]
9. zinc [zɪŋk]
10. think [θʰɪŋk]
11. heart [hɑrt]
12. hard [hɑːrd]
13. hearth [hɑrθʰ]
14. tie [tʰɑɪ]
15. die [dɑɪ]
16. thy [ðɑɪ]
17. thigh [θʰɑɪ]
18. sigh [sʰɑɪ]
19. breath [brɛθʰ]
20. bread [brɛːd]
21. breadth [brɛːdθʰ]

F. (To be carried out like similar exercises done earlier.)

1. (a. thought)(b. taught) I would never have _____ that.
2. (a. booth)(b. boot) That _____ is too small.
3. (a. thinking)(b. sinking) Are you _____ or just lying there?
4. (a. truth)(b. truce) We must have the _____ at all costs.
5. (a. they've)(b. Dave) _____ sat there for hours without moving.
6. (a. these)(b. d's) Can you pronounce _____ perfectly?
7. (a. soothe)(b. sued) He declared he'd _____ her.
8. (a. teething)(b. teasing) I believe the child is only _____.
9. (a. jail)(b. Yale) My son just got out of _____.
10. (a. jet)(b. yet) The color is not _____ black.
11. (a. joke)(b. yolk) I see no _____ in that egg.
12. (a. jeers)(b. cheers) Don't let their _____ disturb you.
13. (a. shin)(b. chin) He hit me on the _____.
14. (a. share)(b. chair) Don't take my _____ from me.
15. (a. dish)(b. ditch) Put the ashes in the _____.
16. (a. washing)(b. watching) What are you _____ so carefully?

G. The sentences in each of the following groups

have the same rhythm and intonation. Repeat
each group until you can produce that particular pattern rapidly and smoothly:

1. a. Can you answer it for me?
   b. Won't you tell us about it?
   c. Is he showing it to them?
   d. You're antagonizing him?
   e. You presented me to her?

2. a. Tom is a great big boy.
   b. Which is the sixteenth floor?
   c. This is a one-man show.
   d. What was in last night's news?
   e. Who has the best bass voice?

3. a. It's a long road that has no turning.
   b. It's a good thing you're not a farmer.
   c. There's a real reason for precautions.
   d. It's a long way to San Francisco.
   e. She was quite happy to be chosen.

4. a. You can't see the forest for the trees.
   b. I don't think there's time for it to
      work.
   c. The sixteenth of August is the day.
   d. A loud "no" was all that he could say.
   e. My old shoes are pleasant to put on.

If facilities are available, the above drill
may be recorded.

H. Read aloud several pages of English, concentrating your attention on avoiding whichever of
the consonant substitutions treated in this
lesson you have noticed in your own speech.

LESSON XV

Consonant Substitutions: II

I. [b], [v], [w], **and** [hw].

These four sounds — [b], [v], [w], and [hw] — form a group within which are made several different substitutions not due to incorrect voicing. Students whose original tongue was Spanish or Tagalog tend to confuse [b] and [v], because of the lack of a clear distinction between the two consonants in those languages; it may seem to an American ear that such students pronounce *visit* as [bɪzɪt] instead of [vɪzɪt]. Scandinavians, Central Europeans, Iranians, members of the Arabic-speaking group, and some others often substitute [v] for [w], give *we* the improper sound of [vi] in place of [wi]. Latin Americans may prefix a [g] to words which begin with [w]; *would* [wʊd] thus becomes [gwʊd]. Since [hw] does not exist in many languages, there is a rather general tendency to replace it in English by [w]; *where* [hwɛər] is mispronounced as [wɛər], *white* [hwaɪt] as [waɪt].

These substitutions are easily made because all four of the sounds — [b], [v], [w], and [hw] — are produced far forward in the mouth, largely with the lips, the teeth, and the tip of the tongue.

You may remember that [b] is a voiced stop, made between the lips. For an initial or medial [b], the lips close firmly, the pressure of air trying to escape builds up briefly behind them, and then the air is released by a sudden opening of the lips: try it with *berry* [bɛrɪ]. In the production of a final [b], the last part of the process, the explosive release of the air as the lips open, is usually not heard (see Lesson VIII, Section III). Can you pronounce *rob* [rɑb], and allow the sound to end while your lips are still closed?

By way of contrast, [v] is a voiced continuant,

[152]

made between upper *teeth* and lower lip. The cutting edge of the upper teeth touches lightly the lower lip, and the air escapes smoothly, without being stopped even momentarily. Neither [b] nor [v] is strongly aspirated, whether in an initial or final position. It should be clear, then, that all that is necessary in order to avoid the [b]-for-[v] substitution is to touch the lower lip against the *teeth* rather than against the upper *lip*. *Very, berry*; [vɛrɪ], [bɛrɪ]; light touch against upper teeth, firm closure of lips.

The [w]-sound is a glide, as is [y]. [w] is essentially a very short and unstressed [u], from which the speaker passes immediately to some full vowel sound. It is heard in words like *went* [wɛnt], and *once* [wəns]. The glide begins with the lips protruded and rounded in the [u]-position (see Lesson XI, Section V); from there the speech organs move on quickly to the position for the following vowel, whatever it may be. In avoiding the [v]-for-[w] substitution, it is most important to protrude the lips and keep the lower lip away from the upper teeth. If this lip even brushes the teeth, the [w] will have some of the [v]-quality about it and may be misunderstood. Contrast *wine* [waɪn] and *vine* [vaɪn], *west* [wɛst] and *vest* [vɛst].

The remaining sound in this group, [hw], is also a glide. It is sometimes known as the "candle-blowing sound," because we make it by emitting a little puff of air through the rounded and protruded lips, just as we do when we want to blow out a candle or match. No such puff of air accompanies the formation of [w]. You can see the difference between these two sounds if you will hold a lighted match about two inches from your lips as you pronounce *witch* [wɪtʃ] and *which* [hwɪtʃ]. *Witch* should hardly cause the flame to flicker, but a properly produced *which* should blow it out.

It should be pointed out that the substitution of [w] for [hw] cannot always be regarded as an error. Good American speakers often make it, especially when pronouncing rapidly such words as *which, where, what, why*, and *when* in unstressed positions. In some forms of British English, [w] for [hw] is common even in stressed words like *whale* and *white*. Such substitutions can result in misunderstanding, however, and it is certainly worthwhile for the student of American English to try to master [hw] in order to achieve as much clarity as possible in his speech.

II. Final [n], [ŋ], and [ŋk].

At the end of words, there is often confusion between [n], [ŋ], and [ŋk]. Some Chinese and Latin American students are accustomed to pronouncing all final n's as [ŋ] in their own language, and find it quite hard not to carry the habit over into English. In their mouths rain [ren] becomes [reŋ], and seen [sin] sounds like [siŋ]. On the other hand, there is another group, especially those whose mother tongue is German or certain of the Central European languages, who often add a [k] to words which should end with an [ŋ]-sound; they pronounce doing [duɪŋ] as [duɪŋk] .

[n], and [ŋ], along with [m], form the group of consonants known as nasals, a classification which we have not so far discussed. In the production of other consonants (orals) the air escapes through the mouth; for the nasals it comes out through the nose. It is the soft palate, or velum, which determines which way the air shall escape. When the velum is drawn up, it closes the nasal passage and forces the air out through the mouth. When the velum is relaxed, the breath stream may pass out either through mouth or nose. To produce a nasal consonant, the velum is relaxed and at the same time the passage through the mouth is blocked at some point by the tongue or lips, so that all the air is forced out through the nose. All normal nasals are voiced. The figures below should help you visualize the essential differences between an oral consonant, [m], [n], and [ŋ].

It will be seen that for [m] the outflow of air through the mouth is blocked by the closing of the lips, for [n] it is blocked by the tongue's touching the tooth ridge, and for [ŋ] by the tongue's bunching in the back of the mouth and pressing against the palate.

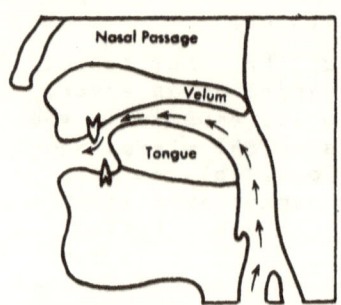

An Oral Consonant

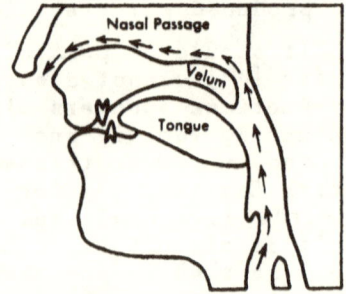

[m]

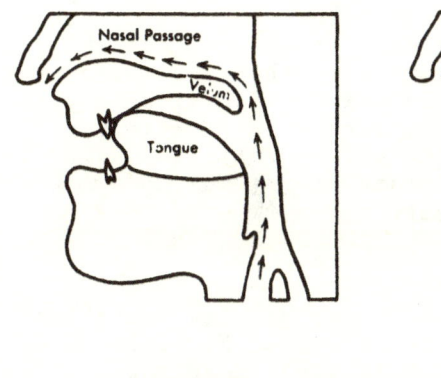
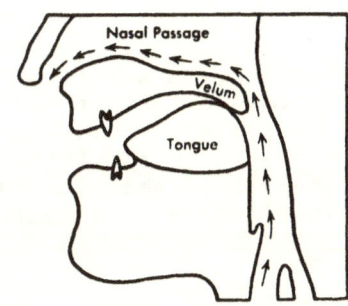

[n]   [ŋ]

To avoid the [ŋ]-for-[n] substitution, then, it is only necessary to see that the tongue tip and blade touch the tooth ridge all around with sufficient firmness to block the escape of air through the mouth. Note the clear contrast in tongue positions for *ran* [ræn] and *rang* [ræŋ], *sin* [sɪn] and *sing* [sɪŋ].

The [ŋk]-for-[ŋ] substitution is a little more difficult to control. One of the causes for it is probably a feeling on the part of the speaker that the final g of a word like *doing* should be pronounced. Since [g] is a voiced sound, a person in whose native language final voiced consonants are not common will tend to substitute for [g] its voiceless counterpart, [k]. It should be understood clearly that the g of the ending -ng is silent; the g changes the preceding n from [n] to [ŋ], but is not itself pronounced. You may be able to realize this fact better if you will note the contrasting pronunciations of *singer* and *finger*. The former is [sɪŋər]; the g is silent, though it affects the sound of n. The latter is [fɪŋgər]; the g not only changes the n, but is also pronounced itself. Can you hear the difference between [ŋ] and [ŋg]? At the end of a word -ng always has the sound of [ŋ], as in *singer*.

You may have noticed that [ŋ], [g], and [k] are all formed with the tongue in the same position, bunched high in the back of the mouth so as to touch the palate. [g] and [k] are oral stops. To produce them the velum is drawn up, preventing the escape of air through the nose. The tongue momentarily blocks the passage of air through the mouth, then releases it explosively. [ŋ] is a nasal continuant. The velum is re-

laxed, allowing the air to pass out through the nose.
The tongue, which blocks the passage through the mouth,
remains in its position until the end of the sound.
There is no explosive release of breath. The [ŋk]-for-
[ŋ] substitution may be avoided, then, by taking care
that there shall be no explosive release, no aspiration, at the end of a word like *rang*. The tongue should
remain pressed against the palate until the sound is
completely finished. Contrast *rang* [ræŋ] and *rank* [ræŋk],
sing [sɪŋ] and *sink* [sɪŋk].

III. [h].

The problem with [h] is not usually substitution,
but omission. It is another of those English sounds
which do not occur in certain other languages, notably
French, Italian, and Portuguese. In Spanish the [h]-
sound exists, but is given to the letter j; the letter
h is always silent. This means that speakers of one of
the Latin languages may have difficulty in producing
[h], and find it natural simply to ignore the sound.

This tendency is probably strengthened by the fact
that in a few common English words the h really should
be left silent: *heir* [ɛər], *honor* [ɑnər], and *hour*
[aur]. Either pronunciation, with or without [h], is
possible for *herb*, [ərb] or [hərb]; *homage*, [hɑmɪdʒ] or
[ɑmɪdʒ]; and *humble* [hə́mbəl] or [ə́mbəl]. Furthermore,
native speakers of English frequently omit the [h] of
little words such as *he, him, his, her, have, has,* and
had, when these are in an unstressed position in the
sentence: *Tell him now* [tɛ́əl ɪm náu]; *We have done it*
[wi əv də́n ɪt].

Except in the cases mentioned above, all initial
h's should be sounded. Even with *he, him,* etc., it is
certainly not necessary to omit the h in order to avoid
a "foreign accent."

[h] is an voiceless continuant, and no particular
position of the tongue and lips is required to produce
it. With the speech organs in the position of the sound
which is to follow [h], the breath is forced through
the partially closed vocal cords and out of the mouth
with sufficient strength to make a rushing sound (as if
the speaker were panting for breath): *home* [hom], *house*
[haus].

IV. Exercises.

    A. 1. Imitate as your teacher pronounces: v-v-v,
v-v-v, v-v-v. Be sure that the cutting edge
of your upper teeth touches your lower lip.

American English Pronunciation 157

    2. a. vɛn   l. ɪnvɑ́ɪt
        b. vɛst   m. various vegetables
        c. vɔɪs   n. overly virtuous
        d. vyu   o. never vexed
        e. vízɪt   p. to verify the victory
        f. vflɪdʒ   q. a vicious savage
        g. ləv   r. a big vote
        h. brev   s. a vivid blue
        i. hɛ́vɪ   t. a very bad verdict
        j. sɛ́vən   u. an oval table
        k. ɪnvɛ́d   v. a back vowel

    3. Without looking at the printed page, repeat this drill rapidly after your instructor. Concentrate on the *thought* of the sentences, and depend on your instructor to call to your attention any mispronounced [v]'s.

        a. I've sealed the envelope.
        b. I've had very little vacation.
        c. I've prevented an accident.
        d. I've never tried to write verse.
        e. I've read Volume I.
        f. I've just left my favorite class.
        g. I've several vices.
        h. I've spilled gravy on my vest.
        i. I've never even seen it.
        j. I've lost some valuable papers.
        k. I've never driven a Packard.
        l. I've learned all vowels are voiced.

B. 1. wi, wi, wi; wɔ, wɔ, wɔ. Be sure your lips are rounded and protruded, and that you keep your lower lip away from your upper teeth.

    2. a. we   k. within a week
        b. wɔl   l. gone with the wind
        c. wɛnt   m. wish me well
        d. wər   n. to waste away
        e. kwɪk   o. to awaken at once
        f. kwaɪət   p. without vigor
        g. swɪm   q. a vast world
        h. ɔ́lwez   r. a loving wife
        i. bɪwɛ́ər   s. vile weather
        j. bɪtwín   t. to win over
                        u. a wicked villain

    3. a. I wish I were a woman.
        b. I wish I had a sandwich.
        c. I wish I weighed less.
        d. I wish I knew more words.
        e. I wish I could find work.

f. I wish I were widely read.
g. I wish we had won.
h. I wish we were through.
i. I wish you would warn us.
j. I wish you would reward us.
k. I wish the window were open.
l. I wish to ask a question.

C. 1. With your hand before your lips, pronounce [we] and [hwe] several times. You should be able to feel the puff of air with which [hwe] is produced.

2.
a. hwaɪ
b. hwat
c. hwɛn
d. hwɪtʃ
e. hwaɪɹ
f. hwɪp
g. hwiəl
h. əhwə́ɹl
i. sə́mhwat
j. ɛ́vrɪhwɛəɹ

k. the white whale
l. which wharf
m. the whip whistled
n. a whiff of whiskey
o. to whine and whimper
p. wherever you wish
q. to wash his whiskers
r. a wild whistle
s. to whisk away
t. while the wind whirled
u. whether we want it or not

3.
a. I know what you want us to do.
b. I know what we're to study.
c. I know what a whirlwind is.
d. I know what you whispered.
e. I know nowhere to look.
f. I know where the laboratory is.
g. I know when we make recordings.
h. I know when I pronounce it right.
i. I know all your whims.
j. I know which bus to take.
k. I know why the wheels turn.
l. I know why we're doing this.

D. 1. Imitate as your teacher pronounces [ræn], [ræŋ], [ræŋk] several times. Be sure that your tongue touches your tooth ridge for [n], your palate for [ŋ], and that there is no explosive release of breath for either sound.

2.

n	ŋ	ŋk
a. sin	g. sing	m. sink
b. thin	h. thing	n. think
c. win	i. wing	o. wink
d. son	j. sung	p. sunk
e. bun	k. bung	q. bunk
f. ban	l. bang	r. bank

3. Read these sentences aloud, making as clear

a distinction as possible between the [n], [ŋ], and [ŋk] of the underscored words:

a. They r<u>an</u> and r<u>ang</u> the bell.
b. A new g<u>ang</u> war beg<u>an</u>.
c. I think he's k<u>in</u> to the k<u>ing</u>.
d. It's p<u>inching</u> my ch<u>in</u>.
e. Come <u>on</u>; get al<u>ong</u>.
f. A pilot must w<u>in</u> his w<u>ings</u>.
g. What are you d<u>oing</u> with the <u>ink</u>?
h. The Titanic's passengers s<u>ang</u> as the ship s<u>ank</u>.
i. Are you <u>ordering drinks</u>?
j. I th<u>ink</u> the th<u>ing</u> is possible.
k. The chains cl<u>ank</u> and cl<u>ang</u>.
l. The flowers are dr<u>opping</u> their p<u>ink</u> petals.

E. 1. h-h-h, h-h-h, h-h-h

2. a. hi   g. hɔrs   m. hard-hearted
   b. hu   h. hit   n. high-handed
   c. haʊs   i. hərt   o. the whole of history
   d. hrər   j. əhɛ́d   p. a happy home
   e. het   k. pərhǽps q. my only hope
   f. hold   l. bɪhév   r. an entire hen

3. Without looking at the printed page, repeat this drill rapidly after your instructor. Concentrate on the *thought* of the sentences, and depend on your instructor to call your attention to the omission of any [h]'s which should not be omitted.

   a. I hear you've been in the hospital.
   b. I hear you have heard from home.
   c. I hear you're going away for the holidays.
   d. I hear you know how to manage a horse.
   e. I hear you hope to be able to hire an automobile.
   f. I hear you've been hesitating to ask for help.
   g. I hear he's been misbehaving.
   h. I hear he always has high grades.
   i. I hear he's not happy here.
   j. I hear he habitually hides his errors.
   k. I hear she has an admirable head of hair.
   l. I hear it has already happened.
   m. I hear they're holding open house.
   n. I hear I must meet the American history and institutions requirement.
   o. I hear that instructor is often harsh.

Consonant Substitutions: II

F.
	b		v		w		hw
1.	bail	7.	veil	13.	wail	19.	whale
2.	buy	8.	vie	14.	Y	20.	why
3.	bile	9.	vile	15.	wile	21.	while
4.	bet	10.	vet	16.	wet	22.	whet
5.	___	11.	vine	17.	wine	23.	whine
6.	best	12.	vest	18.	west	24.	___

G. In order to help fix in your mind the position in which the consonants studied in these last two lessons and the back vowels are formed, another lip-reading exercise is included here. Your instructor will form some of the combinations below with his lips, tongue, etc., without actually uttering any sound. Try to recognize each combination and write down its number.

1. bɑ 4. vɑ 7. wɑ 10. ðɑ 13. dɑ
2. bo 5. vo 8. wo 11. ðo 14. do
3. bə 6. və 9. wə 12. ðə 15. də

H. 1. (a. bow)(b. vow) He made a _____ to greet us cordially.
2. (a. boat)(b. vote) The candidate received a large _____.
3. (a. bat)(b. vat) A _____ is used in making beer.
4. (a. veil)(b. wail) A _____ is a sign of sorrow.
5. (a. verse)(b. worse) It couldn't possible be _____.
6. (a. vines)(b. wines) Californians should know about _____.
7. (a. way)(b. whey) Make _____ for the dairy truck.
8. (a. wetting)(b. whetting) Why are you _____ your knife?
9. (a. ton)(b. tongue) Does it weigh as much as a _____?
10. (a. sin)(b. sing) Don't urge me to _____.
11. (a. stun)(b. stung) Your remarks _____ me.
12. (a. wing)(b. wink) The waitress gave me a _____.
13. (a. sing)(b. sink) The child won't _____ in the water.
14. (a. bang)(b. bank) I wouldn't _____ on the door, if I were you.
15. (a. hitch)(b. itch) I hope no _____ will develop.
16. (a. heart)(b. art) Put your _____ in your work.

17. (a. heating)(b. eating) I won't live there because of the _____ arrangements.

I. This exercise may be the last chance you will get to familiarize yourself with natural intonation patterns by making your voice follow a visible line. As you work on the passage, write in such phonetic symbols and markings as you feel would help you with any pronunciation difficulties you may still be having. The material is suitable for recording.

1. The young man took a watch from his pocket and looked at it. 2. "I guess we'd better make it snappy if we're going to the last show," he said. 3. "Just about ten minutes is all we've got." 4. "Oh," said she. 5. "Where shall we go?" he persisted; "Is there anything special you'd like to see? 6. What's on, anyway; have you got a paper?" 7. "There isn't anything special. 8. I guess I've seen just about everything, as a matter of fact." 9. "Me too."

10. She suggested timidly, "Do we have to go the movies?" 11. "Why, don't you want to?"

12. "If you don't think you'd get tired of me,"

she murmured, "I'd just as soon we stayed

right here like this."

(Adapted from the story "My Sister Frances" by Emily Hahn, originally published in *The New Yorker*.)

J. Read aloud several pages of English, concentrating your attention on avoiding whichever of the consonant substitutions treated in this lesson you have noticed in your own speech.

www.ingramcontent.com/pod-product-compliance
Lightning Source LLC
Chambersburg PA
CBHW021709230426
43668CB00008B/775